A Glorious Nightmare in 64 Shades of Green

By: Gamble Dick

Published by CLC Publishing, LLC.
Mustang, OK 73064

Printed in the United States of America

Book Design by Shannon Whittington
Cover Art by Gamble Dick

ISBN: 9781689138604

Non-Fiction/Military/Vietnam War
Non-Fiction/Military/Special Forces

"We have shared the incommunicable experience of war, we have felt, we still feel, the passion of life to its top. In our youth our hearts were touched with fire." ~ Oliver Wendell Holmes

What began as a few pages for my grandchildren to have as an account of what their grandfather experienced in Vietnam has evolved into this complete work.

To My Grandchildren:

I am writing this for us…for you, so you'll know what I was like and how life was when I was younger; and for me, so I can remember some special people and places.

Brandon has known me since I was about 55 or so. Gavin and Kyle came next, followed by Ella. She thinks I've just always been an old guy. That may be true now, but once upon a time, even before your moms and dads were born, I had some adventures and I was pretty good at what I did. This book is about one of my adventures…my first tour of duty in Vietnam.

There are no grand thoughts or great philosophies here, but there are true stories about some great and courageous men…not famous, but much better than famous. They believed in something greater than themselves and they put their country and their "brothers" before themselves. Although most of them didn't receive any special medals or recognition, there were men of honor. They were heroes.

This is also a "love letter" to the little blind date girl. I wouldn't be here if not for her. Success in life is about good decision-making and the best decision I ever made was to love the little blind date girl. I've had a lot of good days because of her.

I would like to ask a personal favor of each of you: please don't do drugs or smoke…really bad decisions. I would like it if you didn't get tattoos or body piercings, but I know the world is changing, so be discrete. Remember, no matter what you think, there is always someone watching. Be polite and behave yourselves! Make good decisions and good impressions and your lives will be better than mine…and mine was great!

I hope you enjoy this and that it answers, to some degree, any questions you may have about those times in Vietnam and why I am the way I am.

I love each of you the best,

Papa.

Every veteran's war story is a little different. In fact, anyone could have gone through the experience I am about to relate standing right next to me and have a totally different take on it. For me, it was an epic adventure resulting in an enhanced love of country, suspicions and distrust about the government, vast reservoirs of personal confidence and mental toughness, and huge disappointments regarding some of my friends and fellow citizens. I was not just a veteran; I was a combat veteran!

My war story took place in Southeast Asia between the fall of 1967 and the fall of 1970. I am writing about my 1st tour of duty in Vietnam from September 1967 to September 1968. You're not going to believe this shit, which is how all good war stories begin. I was a Special Forces Officer (Green Beret) assigned to a very Top-Secret Operation. It was very exciting, and I am proud of what I did. I never did anything that would bring shame to myself, my family, or my country.

What an experience! I will relate what I remember so that my grandchildren will know about that part of my life if they are ever interested and others who may read this will know that we fought with great courage and dedication. We didn't fight for wealth, fame or territory; we fought to keep a nation from being oppressed and enslaved. That's the Special Forces motto: "De Oppresso Liber", to free the oppressed. Plenty of people and institutions got in the way and corrupted the altruistic nature of our mission but the extraordinary men I served with deserve recognition for their honor, honesty, courage and abilities.

In some respects, coming home was the worst part of my first year in Vietnam. To arrive home to the country I had fought for, and on one or two occasions almost died for, only to receive a back-handed slap from the citizens of the country I loved, hurt me . . . deeply. I think I handled the physical and mental aspects of combat fairly well, maybe even better than most, but I will always carry anger and disappointment over coming home to a thankless, and sometimes hateful, America.

I'm glad I served in Vietnam and I wouldn't trade the experiences for anything. As the saying goes, "If you experienced it, no explanation is necessary, if you didn't, no explanation is possible." I had the privilege of fighting alongside incredibly intelligent, courageous and patriotic men. I fought for my country because I loved and believed in it. I fought for South Vietnam because I believed that freedom offered the Vietnamese a better way of life than that offered by communism. But in the end, I fought for my brothers and the bonds that we built in combat. The days of my first tour were, and remain, a glorious nightmare.

I

October nights in Tucson, Arizona, were almost perfect in 1962. The sweltering summer heat had finally broken, and the "monsoon" season of July and August was long gone, returning the humidity to a very comfortable single digit number. Sitting around a campfire in the desert with my friends and looking at the clear night sky wondering where I would be going and what I would be doing with my life was only made better with a soft, sweet smelling girl resting in the crook of my arm. It was an idyllic time. One that I thought about often in the coming years.

I was born in 1945 in Tucson, Arizona and in 1962/63 I was a senior at Tucson High School. I had a girlfriend, who was a cheerleader at Salpointe, the Catholic high school. She was beautiful and fun, and we spent a lot of time together while our hormones battled our consciences.

The best nights were Friday nights. In the early 60's almost any high school kid in America who had a social life was at the football game with his or her date. I was on the football field under the lights. I stood five feet, nine inches and with all the equipment I was wearing, I might have weighed 155 pounds. I was a backup linebacker/fullback and full-time tackling dummy on the Tucson High School Badgers, one of the best teams in the state.

We were just two games away from playing in the first ever Arizona State High School Football

Championship. We hadn't lost a game and I was proud to be a part of the team and the excitement that came with it. I loved that team and it symbolized so much that was good in America. Our quarterback was Hispanic, smart, athletic and a general all-around good guy. Our fullback was white, tough, and liked by everyone. One of our halfbacks was oriental, not just smart but brilliant. And the other halfback slot was filled by two black guys, one skittered through the opposition like a water bug and the other was a power runner. We were what I thought America was. I was sheltered and naïve.

I played first string on the special teams . . . kick-offs and punts. I had heart and I loved playing on the special teams. There was a lot of speed and smashing into opposing players and if you were the lucky one, you brought the opposing ball carrier down with a solid, bone-jarring crash. I was pumped. Kick off was only a few minutes away.

The "butterflies" had been building all day and as I stepped on the field for the opening kick-off, they peaked. Please God, don't let me make any mistakes. More than anything, I didn't want to let my teammates down.

Here we go! The kicker's foot made contact with the ball for the opening kick-off and the 'butterflies' flew away as I made hard contact with the first opposing blocker. Let the game begin!

We won the game and after the game we hooked up with our girlfriends and a bunch of us went to "Johnnie's" for Cokes, burgers and fries. A perfect Friday night! On Saturdays, we would go to parties or find quiet places to talk and explore our passions for one another. We had very moral upbringings and would never do anything to shame our families, but it was hard for us to resist the temptations.

The Badgers went on to play in the state championship and lost 40 to 7. In the spring I broke a state record in swimming. My grades were good. My senior year of high school was innocent and euphoric as was the summer following my high school graduation. I had another wonderful summer with my girl and my buddies. We went water-skiing and jumped the fence at the Racquet Club for midnight swims. We picnicked in the mountains and cruised Speedway like a thousand other kids.

Suddenly it was time for all of us to go to college and my girl left for an exclusive girl's college in Virginia. I went to the University of Arizona because it was all I could afford. It was only a few weeks later that I was set up with a really cute girl from Topeka, Kansas. It was fun showing her around and I got too involved too quickly.

Before I knew it, Christmas was upon us and I realized I had a female management problem. "Virginia" was flying into Tucson on the same plane that "Kansas" was leaving on to go home. I took Kansas to the airport to say good-bye and as the incoming plane taxied to the terminal, I excused myself and went to the men's room where I stayed until I was sure Kansas had departed. Not my finest moment and I am ashamed of myself to this day.

Tactically it was a good move and solved my immediate problem. Strategically it was a total failure and I found myself girlfriendless by February and I remained that way for several years. I found other things to do, that to me, were as compelling as romance. Time to get on with my life!

Another October five years later. It was steam iron hot and humid, and the idyllic life I had lived in Tucson was far behind me. I was a Special Forces Officer (Green Beret) assigned to SOG, the Studies and Observation Group, and further assigned to Forward Operating Base 1 in Phu Bai, South Vietnam, a few miles south of Hue. We were part of the "Black Ops" efforts of the war in Vietnam.

"You've never lived until you've almost died; for those who have fought for it, life has a flavor the protected will never know." ~ SOG saying...author unknown

SOG was a complex Top-Secret organization with many classified programs involving both conventional and unconventional warfare activities in Southeast Asia. Many of the activities were passed from the CIA to the military as the war progressed and expanded. Others were generated by the importance of, and need for, information about the "Troung Son Strategic Supply Route" or as we knew it, the "Ho Chi Minh Trail", or just the "Trail."

Members and units assigned to SOG were drawn from all branches of the U.S. Military. There were specialized Maritime Operations (OP-31), Air Operations (OP-32), Psychological Operations (OP-

33), and a number of Ground Operations and Projects (Op-34...Long Term Agent Training and Operations, Op-35...Ground Operations, and Projects Delta, Gamma, Omega, and Sigma). I was assigned to OP-35, the cross border ground reconnaissance operation.

Responsibilities of OP-35, in addition to basic reconnaissance and reporting, were directing air-strikes against observed targets, rescuing downed pilots and others missing in action (known as "Bright Light" operations), capturing enemy troops and equipment, assisting with Psychological Operations, and conducting raids or ambushes against specified locations or targets.

Between 1964 and 1972, when OP-35 was active, an estimated 2000 to 2500 U.S. personnel were assigned to the project. Seven to eight thousand Vietnamese ethnic minorities (Nungs [Vietnamese-Chinese], Cambodians from the various clans, my Cambodes were Kymer Kompuchea Krom [KKK], and Montagnards) serving as paramilitary mercenaries rounded out the complement.

Cross-border Operations started in 1964 using Vietnamese Special Forces venturing into Laos and a small contingent of American Advisors who were forbidden to leave the political boundaries of South Vietnam. By the fall of 1965, it was obvious that the intelligence provided by the Vietnamese teams was unreliable. The need for good information about the Communist's activities in Laos, Cambodia, and on the "Trail" resulted in U.S. Special Forces personnel leading the reconnaissance teams into Laos and later,

Cambodia. We would waste precious lives bringing back reliable first-hand intelligence information only to have it ignored or ridiculed by the brass in Saigon because it didn't fit their agenda. Exciting but frustrating work.

Although SOG was authorized to conduct operations in Laos and Cambodia by the Presidents of the United States and South Vietnam, plans for our missions would have to wend their way through the Department of Defense and then through the Department of State before getting final approval. Then Ambassador William Sullivan, the U. S. Ambassador to Laos, would impose his own layer of approval and further restrict the rules of engagement. His desires to preserve the neutrality of Laos, reduce "peripheral" damage, and keep the Soviet Union and China from reacting to a U.S. military presence there, often resulted in dangerous delays or restrictions placed on SOG operations. He was called the "Field Marshall" by many and was rumored to have a very close relationship with Boris Kornissovsky, the Russian Ambassador to Laos.

Ambassador Sullivan was not the only one concerned with the Soviet and Chinese reactions. That consideration colored most of the major political decisions involving America's prosecution of the overall war in Vietnam. In the case of Laos and Cambodia, it seemed to be an unnecessary concern since the North Vietnamese Army, also known as PAVN, the People's Army of Vietnam, with Soviet and Chinese advisors, operated there openly, although they denied it. Souvanna Phouma, the Premier of

Laos, supported U.S. involvement and assistance, though not necessarily openly. His regime was fighting the Communist Pathet Lao forces for control of Laos. Politics and diplomacy hindered military operations throughout the war and most of us who were fighting the war felt confident that if we were allowed to fight the war the way wars should be fought, we would see total victory in 6 months.

I was assigned to a Hatchet Force, a platoon-sized element of mercenary soldiers. I would be going into the dark, mysterious lands west of the Vietnam border, known as "Indian Country".

My first mission over "the fence" into "Indian Country" (Laos) came about because Captain Joe Bane and 1st Lieutenant Gene Silver were away from camp. They normally commanded the Nung Company. My roommate, Bill Vowell, and I were assigned to the Cambodian Company but we got the nod to lead this mission with the Nungs. The Nungs were ethnic Chinese born in Vietnam and were good troops. Most of the recon teams were staffed with well-trained Nungs and the Nungs in training were assigned to the company.

I was not part of the planning. I was given a map and told we were going into the northwest side of the A Shau Valley across the Laotian border. The northwest side of Ashau Valley was probably the hottest area in Vietnam. It was where Route 922 and many smaller trails fed into South Vietnam from the principle Ho Chi Minh trail. The area was all important to the NVA and they protected it with a fervor not seen elsewhere in

Vietnam. It was the one area the U.S. military never truly controlled.

Intelligence gleaned from one of our recon teams indicated that there were bunkers in the area where we were going. If there were bunkers, then something was being protected and we would be tasked with trying to find it.

The Ho Chi Minh trail was crucial to North Vietnam's ability to wage war in the South. Building the trail started in 1959 and was a major engineering feat. Originally a system of foot trails and bicycle paths sufficed, but when the U.S. entered the war, the trail became a series of roads and pipelines that ultimately moved 10,000 trucks a night. To protect the trail from aerial surveillance, trees and bushes were trellised over the trail and plants in planter boxes would be moved on the trail during the daytime.

It is estimated that thousands of NVA troops were dedicated to the protection and maintenance of the trail.

A Shau Valley was known to American troops as "Death Valley". It was the most heavily defended enemy stronghold in South Vietnam . . . and it was terrifying! "Hamburger Hill" was there; Firebase "Rip Cord" was there, and they were without doubt, some of the worst battles of the war.

A Shau was plagued with rain, mist and low ceilings most of the year. Here the monsoon never really ended. The weather frequently precluded air support and resupply which were mainstays of the

American effort. That made it doubly dangerous. Below the mist and overcast were trails and bunkers with interlocking fields of fire that had been years in the making. NVA troops garrisoned the area by the tens of thousands.

Large defoliated trees reached up through the mist like skeletal arms and hands waiting to pluck helicopters and planes from the sky with the help of many anti-aircraft guns. I had many occasions to fly into or over the northern A Shau and it was about as scary as it gets. The tracers from the bigger guns looked like basket balls but at least if you saw them you'd know they weren't going to hit you. After some of the flights into A Shau and its immediate environs, it wasn't uncommon to be eliminating seat cushion for several days.

According to what I had learned during my training, the communist forces traditionally operated in 3-man groups at the small unit level and many of the groups would be positioned near most potential landing zones to engage and slow down infiltrating forces until more help could arrive. That was the enemy's first line of defense in protecting the trail. Next were larger enemy units stationed along the trail for maintenance and security. Third were the many units passing through on their way to battlefields in South Vietnam.

October 31, 1967, dawned bright and clear, unusual for that time of year. On average, there were only eight dry days in October and nine dry days in November in the target areas in the mountains of Laos.

Perhaps the good weather was a good omen. My experiences would quickly disabuse me of such ideas

I awoke with a bad case of "butterflies" . . . on steroids. This was not high school and it was not a game. It was the real deal. Please God don't let me make any mistakes. More than anything, I don't want to fail my soldiers. A mistake here could cost lives. This was SOG, the Studies and Observation Group, and it raised leadership and responsibility to a whole new level. I learned to revel in it.

For this mission we had a mix of Vietnamese Air Force Kingbees (Old H-34's flown by Vietnamese pilots who had cut their teeth flying for the French) and U.S. Hueys for the insertion. Bill went in first in a Kingbee and I went in last in a Huey. We did have a couple of A-1 Skyraiders on station over the Landing Zone (LZ). The LZ was a small potato, or maybe a Taro, field. It could only take one chopper at a time. Bill had contact with the enemy immediately. The area was guarded by local security troops and their mission, in addition to tilling the soil and building trails, was to engage enemy forces to slow them down and alert other NVA forces in the area.

The higher-ups were all excited about using tear gas in the field and that was most likely the real reason for the mission. They dropped tear gas on the initial insertion; to what effect I have no idea because it had dissipated by the time I hit the ground.

There was a lot of gunfire as the Huey I was in approached the LZ and my butterflies were now as big as fruit bats. I don't know what I expected, but I was surprised that the gunfire sounded like popcorn popping. I assumed it was outgoing fire to cover our landing until a round hit the door frame next to my head. My butterflies flew away. We were only about eight feet off the ground, so I jumped. With all the weight I was carrying, I landed really hard. My butterflies were all gone.

My interpreter saw me jump and immediately followed. He was hit in the foot or broke his ankle as a result of his jump, but either way he was out of the fight immediately. He landed about 10 feet from me. I checked him out and his foot was pretty mangled. I got on the radio and requested the last chopper return for wounded. I picked him up in a "fireman's carry" and headed to where the chopper was waiting 20 to 30 feet away. Thirty feet isn't far, but I still had on my rucksack and he still had on his rucksack. Two "rucks" and a body is a lot of extra weight! I was running as hard as I could in what seemed like slow-motion. I saw the crew-chief motioning me forward and a bullet hit the dirt between the chopper and me and sent up a geyser of dry, loamy dirt.

I'm sure it only took me a few seconds to reach the chopper, but it seemed like a lifetime. I rather unceremoniously dumped my interpreter on the floor of the chopper and stepped back. I was really exhausted from just a few seconds of exertion. I watched the chopper lift off, oblivious to the few rounds that were hitting the dirt near me. Now we only had one interpreter for sixty some odd Nung troops.

I'm ashamed that I don't remember the wounded interpreter's name. He was young and smart and always happy. He arrived back in camp at Phu Bai several months later. He walked with a severe limp, but he always had a big smile for me and constantly thanked me. He married a beautiful young girl who worked in our club and she always gave me free cokes and called me Dai Uy (Captain). I really hope they lived happily ever after.

As soon as the last chopper lifted off the shooting stopped. The A-1's had a couple of 250 pound dumb bombs left, so Bill had them drop on a nearby hilltop in the direction we were going. It was cool to watch. The sky was clear and blue and the A-I's would wing over and dive toward the hilltop. As soon as the bomb released they would pull up sharply and twist and turn (called "jinking") to spoil the aim of any enemy gunners. The bomb would hit and the sound wouldn't reach us for a few seconds. It didn't sound like the movies…it was just a WHAM! I think they dropped four bombs total and departed to the west. Then it was just Covey, the Forward Air Controller, and us.

We started toward the area where the bombs had been dropped. The brush was thick, lush and green at the bottom of the hills where the streams ran. Almost immediately we found a well maintained trail…wide, hard packed, in places there were steps and hand rails, with tall bushes growing over it so it couldn't be seen from the air. We came to a stream which had a bamboo bridge across it. The bridge was about 8 inches under the surface of the water. Anyone flying over would probably not see it due to the depth of the bridge and the reflection of sunlight on the water. We faced a clever enemy and we were obviously deep in his territory.

We climbed to the hilltop to check out the bombing results. There was no doubt that we had trackers following us. They would hit bamboo sticks together to signal each other. It was a little un-nerving. Clouds started moving in during the afternoon and Covey returned to base (RTB). We snaked and slithered down a ridge, crossed a stream and climbed up the next ridge several times that day. The movement was difficult due to the steepness of the terrain. There were lots of indications of enemy presence.

As we moved up the ridges, the thick underbrush gave way to true triple canopy jungle. I had read about the jungle in books and had seen a few pictures, but I was awestruck by the real thing. There were huge trees, teak and mahogany most likely, whose leaves sprouted out over a hundred feet from the jungle floor. At approximately the 50 to 80 foot level was a middle canopy of leaves from smaller trees, and 30 feet or so over our heads was a sparse layer of leaves from scattered saplings. It was dark in this tropical jungle… like sunset and there was no underbrush because of the lack of sunlight. Movement was relatively easy except for the steep sides of the ridges. No saguaros and mesquite trees here. I was a world away from Arizona. It was also hot and humid and we were all soaking wet from our sweat.

Under the triple canopy, it got dark really early. We were moving along a ridge line when we decided to settle in for the night. The sides of the ridge were very steep so we setup in a long, very narrow oval. I nestled into an area between the roots of a large jungle tree, the kind I had here-to-for only seen in pictures. It was probably decades old. The roots were about a foot thick at ground level and dropped down from about eight feet up. They were solid and I felt safe.

I sat up for a while listening to the jungle sounds as they slowly died out and complete darkness took over. I was deprived of sight and my other senses were reduced to minimal input. I reflected on the day. My adventure was really beginning; everything was new and strange, and eventually the dark crept into my heart. I wasn't scared, but I was lonely. I thought about home and my family, the girl I would marry and how much was at risk, not just personally, but also for my soldiers and the people who lived here. I thought about the veterans my family knew and how we revered their service without understanding what they really went through. The night became silent, which was good because it meant nothing was moving around and I drifted into a very light sleep. I awoke at every sound.

During the night, the trackers would make a little noise to get the Nungs to fire and give away our positions. The Nungs had no fire discipline and there was no stopping them. When one fired, they all fired. It was an impressive firepower demonstration. No doubt it helped guide more enemy troops into the area. Everyone in the area knew we were there. They also knew we had serious firepower.

One of the weapons carried by a few of the Nungs was the M-79 Grenade Launcher which we called the "Thumper" because of the sound it made. The M-79 Grenade Launcher fires a 40mm high explosive round and the spinning round must travel about 28 feet before it becomes armed. When the Nungs fired the M-79's in the dark they hit trees as often as not. I could hear the rounds bouncing around without exploding because they hadn't traveled far enough to become armed. By morning, the area had been liberally seeded with egg-sized grenades in various stages of being armed.

It finally became light enough to move out, slowly at first, to avoid kicking or stepping on the M-79 rounds. SFC "Davey" Crockett, a Demolitions Man, left behind some discouragement in the form of a couple of hand grenades with time pencils (small tubes containing vials of acid which eat through a barrier and activate the fuse in a specified period of time) and some "Toe Poppers" (the "Toe Popper" is a small anti-personnel mine designated M-2. When stepped on, it severely injures the foot and lower leg. It is an insidious device that shows no mercy to man or beast.)

As soon as we started moving, there was a clacking sound, definitely man-made, from our back trail. It was a tracker hitting his pieces of bamboo together. It was answered by similar sounds to our left, right, and front. I felt we were now facing at least 12 or more enemy. (The Communist insurgents traditionally operated in three man units.)

We'd been moving about 15 minutes when the first of Davy Crockett's grenades went off. There were several more to no apparent effect. Then we heard a "Toe Popper" and heard the effect…poor guy. That slowed them down a bit.

Throughout the morning the trackers kept signaling each other. It was a tactic the NVA used to drive a unit into an ambush. We changed direction several times to make it harder for the NVA to concentrate in our direction of travel and ambush us.

For food, the Americans carried C-Rations (canned food) or MRE's (Meals, Ready to Eat) which were dehydrated rations in plastic pouches. About half an hour before mealtime, it was recommended that hot water be added to the dried food to reconstitute it. We had no hot water of course, so cold had to do most of the time. The indigenous troops had their own rations which were mostly rice. It was also dehydrated, but they would rehydrate it before going on a mission and carry it in long sausage shaped plastic pouches. They had foil envelopes of condiments which included dried peppers, squid, and octopus. It was their custom to tie a length of parachute cord to the ends of the "sausage" and sling it over their neck. That way they could slit a small opening in the "sausage" and snack all day long.

Apparently the Nungs wanted to try MRE's, so a lot of them had MRE's on this mission. Despite our best advice, they began snacking on the dehydrated rations as they moved through the jungle. They thought the MRE's were "Numba 10" (BAD). Without adding water, the peas and beans were like pieces of gravel and the meat and carrots weren't much better.

We had been moving on a ridge line most of the morning listening to the trackers clacking away. Clouds had moved in and the humidity was building. It was hot and we were all soaked with sweat. We were running short on water. (Water was absolutely critical and was often in short supply, even during the rainy seasons.)

About mid-day we dropped off the ridge and crossed a large stream which was chest deep in some places. I was wearing my Gas Mask Carrier strapped around my waist and tied to my thigh. It got soaked but I didn't think much about it.

Everyone refilled their canteens. The Americans dutifully dropped several iodine tablets in each canteen of stream water to purify it. Many of the Nungs were sucking up water like camels at an oasis, which I thought was odd. They were accustomed to demanding jungle marches and going long periods without water.

About a half hour later we found out why. The Nungs who had been snacking on the dehydrated rations had sucked up a lot of water to quench their abnormal thirst and now the MRE's were rehydrating in their stomachs. When you put a hand on their bellies, it was like feeling a baby kicking in the womb. We took a long break while they threw up. Clack, clack, clack...the trackers must have wondered what was going on. We moved up on another ridge where we spent another dark night with the Nungs occasionally bouncing grenades off trees. A lot of the Nungs had used up, or thrown away, their rations, so we spread our food around.

The next morning we headed out. We hadn't seen much sign of enemy activity for over a day, but we had a brief encounter with some of the trackers when we changed direction and caught a couple of them unaware. A little gunfire was exchanged. Gunships were overhead and dropped teargas to "help us break contact." I put on my gas mask and took a deep breath. Nothing! It was like trying to suck air through wet concrete. I should have dried my mask. I was suffocating.

I ripped my mask off and took a deep breath…of tear gas. Instant blindness and buckets of snot! That is some awful stuff! I was doing the "funky chicken" and running in circles until I could finally see again. One of the Nungs was grabbing me and trying to give me his gas mask. I kept waving him off while he did the "funky chicken". The gas finally drifted off and we looked at each other and started laughing. I felt a real surge of affection for these brave little guys and realized that they had surreptitiously assigned each American a body guard and this guy was trying to take care of me at great risk to himself.

We climbed higher and the terrain became dryer. The triple canopy faded away to double and single canopy with bamboo and dried grass. We started down the other side of a high ridge, snaking our way to the bottom. We took a break about midway down the ridge in some bamboo and dry grass and a party of trackers walked up on the rear of our column.

A nasty little firefight broke out and the Nungs, true to their habit, let fly in all directions. There were bullets everywhere. I quickly learned to dislike gunfights in bamboo. The bullets and fragments were bad like they were in any gunfight but the bamboo didn't fragment like normal forest trees. It shredded into lots of little filaments that cut, like paper cuts. Nothing serious as far as blood loss but infection was almost a certainty.

In an attempt to mark our position for Covey, someone tossed a smoke grenade which started a fire. So while we were beating back the NVA, we were also beating out an impressive little grass fire. We had some wounded and I assume the NVA did also. I was in the middle of the column and never saw much of what was going on.

We loaded up the wounded, called for an evacuation helicopter, and started looking for a spot where we could land a helicopter. There weren't any. It was tough moving the wounded down the hill. It was really steep and we fell as much as walked to the bottom of the ridge. At the bottom there were two bomb craters fairly close together, the vegetation was sparse but there were numerous saplings so the Kingbee could hover about 20 feet above us but couldn't land.

Much to my dismay, when the Kingbee came to a hover, out rappelled Captain "Hero". Be still my heart, we were saved! He was a "Mustang" (promoted up through the ranks or field promoted) who had probably been passed over for Major and desperately needed a medal to get back in the game. He was also a jerk!

The Kingbee had a hoist and we hoisted out the wounded. A light rain started and we moved to the top of a near-by hill, led by the intrepid Captain "Hero".

It was going to be dark soon. We sent a party back to the bomb craters with empty canteens to get water from the bottom of the craters since it wasn't raining hard enough to collect rainwater and Captain "Hero" hadn't thought to bring any additional food or water with him. We now had an extra mouth to feed so we split up the last of our rations for the evening meal.

After we settled in, one of the Nungs gestured emphatically for an M-79. He popped a round down the hill at a bush and the bush let out a scream. They were close tonight. It was going to be a long night and the rain started coming down harder.

I was a long way from home. One of the things I loved most about my distant desert was the way it smelled when it rained; fresh and sweet. Rain in the jungles and   mountains of Southeast Asia just smelled wet and decayed. It was a dreary odor that intensified the feeling of dread one got when staring at the jungle as the light faded.

Bill was plotting locations for "Sky Spots". There was little chance that air support would come to our aid during the night in the rain, but if we relayed 8 digit coordinates to the Air Force, they could enter them into their bombing computers. The computers took into account many variables, including average wind-speed and direction, to determine a point in the sky that the aircraft must release its ordinance to hit the coordinates Bill was plotting.

Eventually a fighter-bomber would arrive in the area above the clouds and fly an azimuth (compass heading) until he reached a spot in the sky where two computed radar beams intersect and he would "pickle" (drop) his ordinance. The bombs would fall thousands of feet through rain and swirling winds and hopefully detonate on or near the coordinates Bill has transmitted to "Alleycat", one of the night-time airborne command posts for coordinating air assets in the night skies over Laos.

Normally "Sky Spots" were not authorized within 2000 meters of friendly personnel…and that's when the wind was much more predictable. With the winds being so unpredictable, there was a chance the bombs could land on us.

It was absolutely black with no ambient light (moon, stars) at all and the rain covered any sound the NVA was making. About 0200 hours Bill called for a spare radio battery. He was only about 30 feet away, but it took me at least twenty minutes to find him. I beat myself up walking into trees and tripping over Nungs. It left bruises. I didn't even try to find my way back to my position and spent the rest of the night sitting in the soaking rain about 10 feet from Bill, listening to him talking to "Alley Cat". At one point, the bombs landed really close. That night was the definition of "sleepless".

It continued raining lightly and misting into the morning and the ceiling was low. There would be no air cover or resupply in these conditions. "Captain Hero" went off to seek his glory taking Bill's radio with my spare battery. My radio was very weak because the original battery was just about out of juice. Bill and I stayed put. We all had the feeling that NVA strength had increased and knew we would have further contact when we moved.

Sure enough, bang, bang, boom. "Hero" came scampering back with a nick on his neck and less one of the Nungs who had gone with him. He had encountered the NVA about 30 meters outside our perimeter. His weapon had misfired, the Nungs had engaged (and one was killed) while "Captain Hero" pulled the pin on a grenade and rolled it toward a visible NVA. "Hero" had a small nick on his neck probably from shrapnel from his grenade. He was lucky!

You'd think an old combat hand like "Hero" would know enough to eject a round from the chamber and throw it away each morning in case overnight moisture had somehow damaged the primer. I knew to do it and this was my first time out.

We radioed Covey that "Playboy" (his personal call sign) was wounded. There was great concern back at the FOB. They were mighty relieved to find out it was only a scratch. They didn't ask about the Nungs, or Lieutenants Vowell (Amphibian) or Dick (Lancer). The guys in the rear area all agreed that "Hero" had been very brave and he would be awarded a Silver Star and a Purple Heart for this action. Maybe he would make Major after all.

The weather cleared enough the next morning to get aircraft into our area, so we set off again along a ridge line that, according to Covey, had a bomb crater that might serve as a one aircraft Landing Zone. This time I was toward the front, about three men behind the point. Ssszzt! The bullet passed by my head so closely that I could feel its heat!

It hit the Nung behind me in the neck and I grabbed him as he was going down. Fortunately there wasn't much blood so I figured it had missed the carotid artery, but the poor guy was going into shock. His eyes were rolled back and his complexion was really yellow and waxy. The medic was right there. (I wish I'd gone on to be a Medic instead of going to OCS. The Special Forces Medics really impressed me.) I remember I said, "You'd better look at him, Doc. He doesn't look so good." It was one of the dumbest things I had ever said.

I was pretty sure the bullet had been meant for me and I figured the NVA had had time to move in some snipers. Bad news! About six Nungs hosed down the trail to our front and we moved out, reaching the bomb crater several minutes later. Again, too many small trees to land a chopper, so Davey Crockett, the Demolitions Sergeant, set about blowing down the bigger trees with explosives. The rest of us fired randomly at the hillsides to discourage the NVA from getting too close. They fired back occasionally.

The first chopper dropped food and ammo and lowered a chain saw and a can of gas by rope. We were getting the trees out of the way in a hurry now. I was starved, so I grabbed a can of Chicken and Noodles; I opened it, and sat at the edge of the bomb crater eating. I heard a couple rounds smacking into the mud nearby but I was too hungry and too tired to care.

In a few minutes choppers started landing one at a time and we were hustling Nungs on board, including the Nung who was wounded in the neck. He looked much better. I gave him a "thumbs up" and he smiled weakly. We were high in the mountains and the choppers were struggling. They would lift up enough to hover to the edge of the ridge and then literally fall down the mountain to gain enough speed to fly. I held my breath a couple of times but everyone was making it. Finally Bill made me get on a chopper and away I went. He took the last chopper.

Bill said they rigged the stuff we left behind, mostly grenades and a gas can, to explode several minutes after he left in the last chopper. They circled to watch and he said several NVA were going through the stuff when it blew up!

The flight back was unremarkable, but long. It made me realize how far we were from any support when we were "across the fence". We landed at FOB 1 and unloaded. The troops made a B-line for camp to dump their "rucks" and get some chow.

I stood on our LZ at FOB 1 waiting for Bill on the last chopper and I waited and waited. I was afraid something bad had happened, but they had stopped to refuel before returning to the FOB. It reminded me just how far out we had been. Finally the last chopper landed about twenty minutes behind everyone else. Those pilots had pushed their birds to the limit that day.

Off Bill and I went to get our traditional post-mission steak and eggs! Bill left for Saigon the next day for debriefing. I tried to catch up on my sleep and clean up my gear.

As first missions go, this one had met all my expectations and I learned some important lessons. For one thing, I added a "Banana" knife (a small machete) to my gear so I could chop down small trees when the need arose. I also decided that another quart of water would be worth the additional weight. I got rid of my White Phosphorous grenade which was heavy and useless.

II

An awful lot had happened to me between October 1962 and October 1967.

I graduated high school in 1963. My senior year in high school I was President of the Letterman's Club and did pretty well academically (I was a member of the National Honor Society and graduated 75th in a class of 497). I was fortunate to have slightly above average intelligence and athletic ability.

My family could not afford to send me to college, so with the help of an Honor Society scholarship, I paid my own way to the University of Arizona working 2 jobs. I tried to be the guy I thought my family and friends wanted me to be but it really was kind of boring. I even tried a fraternity, but I wasn't part of that world and dropped out of the fraternity after a semester of dismal grades and no money. I was not motivated and had no passion for any of the academic offerings. After three semesters it was pretty clear that I was wasting the University's time. I wasn't focused in that direction. I wanted adventure! I really wanted to be part of the Vietnam War experience to see if I had what it took. Leaving college helped me make a decision about it.

The conflict in Vietnam was beginning to dominate the nightly news and the newspaper headlines. I thought about it a lot. I was young and naïve! I never imagined that the government and the press would routinely lie to the public and that the war would be prosecuted in Washington, D.C. by two incompetent politicians (Johnson and McNamara) who had no experience as warfighters. Nor did I think the people in the country I loved would fail to support their Military and eventually come to revere their traitors and revile the men and women in uniform. It never occurred to me that the U.S. media would become one of the mightiest weapons in the enemy's arsenal. At the time I was nineteen years old and blissfully unaware of all the evil and corruption in the world.

Our country had bested the Soviets in their attempted blockade of Berlin and the free world had fought Communism to a stalemate in Korea barely a decade before. Castro had recently declared Cuba to be Communist and the USSR had tried to place medium range nuclear missiles there, bringing the world to the brink of nuclear disaster. Khrushchev was promising to bury us and the spread of Communism through Soviet supported "Wars of Liberation" was a very real threat to freedom around the world. The "Domino Theory" was still credible and I grew up believing that Communism was every bit as evil as Fascism and Nazism. Stopping it seemed like a worthwhile endeavor. I, like many people, saw the conflict in Vietnam as another battle in the "Cold War".

In addition, the U.S. was a member of SEATO, the Southeast Asia Treaty Organization. At the time I believed that our word was our bond and we were obligated to send support to our ally, the Republic of South Vietnam. In my mind, we sought no territory, no treasure, and we did not want to impose our way of life on the South Vietnamese. I believed we just wanted to assure their freedom to choose their own way of life. I believed our motives were purely altruistic and our cause was noble, or at least mine were.

A few years earlier President John F. Kennedy famously said, "Ask not what your country can do for you, but what you can do for your country." I decided to answer the call.

At the time, I was working at Tucson Medical Center as a surgical orderly. I liked it and it was interesting, and occasionally exciting, but I yearned for something more. I was seriously thinking about enlisting in the Marine Corps so I could go to Vietnam with an elite fighting unit.

On my twentieth birthday, my mother, who always gave me books, gave me "The Green Berets" by Robin Moore...and there was the answer. I was going to be a Special Forces Medic. I enlisted in the United States Army several months later. The only promise the recruiter made was that I would get a chance to be Airborne, a Para-trooper. He could not promise that I would make it into Special Forces, but I was motivated and willing to take a chance.

I wasn't your stereotypical recruit, at least not the one that the media portrayed. I was not drafted. It is a common misconception that most of the men who fought in Vietnam were drafted. While that was true in World War II, only a third of the men who fought in Vietnam were draftees. 70% of the 58,148 members of the U.S. Military who were killed in Vietnam were volunteers...of course many people enlisted to avoid being placed in the infantry. But really, if you are in the Army and you're not an Infantryman it's a lot like having the hottest girl in school in your bed and all you do is cuddle.

I was not terribly "conflicted" about what the U.S. was trying to do in South Vietnam. I believed in stopping the spread of Communism and keeping our treaty obligations. I wanted to be in the action. I was very naive.

In September of 1965, I departed for Basic and Advanced Infantry Training at Fort Polk, near Leesville, Louisiana (known affectionately as Fort Puke near Diseaseville, Louisiana).

Training was a unique experience, a great equalizer. Young men from all corners of the country and all walks of life came together to participate in one of life's great passages. I feel sorry for men who didn't experience it.

I marveled at the Drill Sergeants who systematically broke us down as individuals, taught us new skills, and built us back with all sorts of here-to-for unknown information and abilities regarding life in general and war fighting in particular. We became improved versions of our former selves.

It all started with a haircut and olive drab clothes. We temporarily lost our individuality and the west coast surfers, the east coast city boys and all the farmers and ranchers in between just looked like kids with bad haircuts and no fashion sense. We banded together for self-preservation from the constant onslaught of the Drill Sergeants and our Team began to form.

We became faster and stronger and realized we were better together than as individuals. We developed skill and pride and life-long friends. There were some bad times and we helped each other through them. And there were funny times. One of my favorite memories was of Dave, who bunked next to me. He was hard and lanky and a really good guy. He came from back in the hills of Missouri and was acutely aware his education had been lacking. He got teased (not bullied) and usually reacted with anger.

Before chow each evening we had cleaning details and one evening Dave and I were assigned to rake the low crawl pit, a 25-yard long sand pit that we routinely low-crawled through for the entertainment of our training staff. I'm sure we provided the Drill Instructors with endless amusement.

It is the custom at all Army bases to sound "Taps", a bugle call signifying that "Day is done" at the end of the duty day. "Taps" is sounded throughout the base over the loud speakers and all personnel stop whatever they are doing and face the flag at post headquarters and render a salute until "Taps" ends. Dave and I were raking the pit when "Taps" sounded. We both snapped to attention and faced in the direction of post headquarters. I dropped my rake and rendered a sharp salute. Dave wasn't sure what to do about the rake so he came to "present rake." I couldn't help myself and started to giggle. Dave was not pleased and started after me while swinging his rake. The second time around the barracks he started laughing and by the third lap we were totally winded and walking together back to the pit. Small vignettes like this brought us together and we developed the kinds of friendships that result in unbreakable bonds and brotherhood. I can't explain it, and it seems stupid, but I know I became one of those guys. To this day I would take a bullet for Dave or hundreds of other guys with whom I served.

As a result of the Drill Sergeants' efforts I became a member of an organization that was larger than the sum of its parts. It demanded honor and courage. I felt pride in what I was becoming.

The training not only made us soldiers but it escalated us into manhood and taught us about the serious aspects of life on our planet. As much as I learned "How to" I learned just as much about "How not to", by watching those around me, especially the officers.

Every Saturday morning we had barracks inspections by the Company Commander or Executive Officer. On one particular Saturday successfully passing inspection was to result in off-post pass privileges. We went all out. One of the rules of the inspection was that we had an "honor" wall locker and footlocker that were exempt from inspection where we could stash last minute items and cleaning supplies. The barracks looked sharp and when Lt. Petulant Child, the Company XO, entered we snapped to attention. He began his inspection of our uniforms, wall lockers and footlockers. He found nothing amiss even though he tried really hard. As he was leaving he opened the exempt lockers even though he was honor bound not to. There was an orange in the footlocker.

He had a screaming fit, threw the orange on the floor and it splattered everywhere. He had us fall out for physical punishment for having contraband in the barracks. Needless to say we were confined to the post for the weekend. For me, it was a great learning experience. It showed me how not to be an officer and I swore that I would never do anything that chicken shit. Several weeks later he was gone.

When I had entered the Army at the Reception Depot, part of my in-processing had been to take a battery of tests and I did well, qualifying for Special Forces and Officer Candidate School. I decided on Officer's training and Lt. Petulant Child had given me my first lesson.

In Officer Candidate School (OCS) I got lots of "officer lessons" and 99% of them were good, common sense leadership. Our Tactical (TAC) Officers were young Lieutenants and with an exception or two, were really good guys with a serious job to do. The exception in my Company was a TAC Officer with serious "little man" syndrome. One day we were at the Mortar Range and if we weren't actively engaged in firing one of the Mortars we observed from the bleachers. The Georgia summer could be dangerous and it was a "Red Flag" day, meaning to minimize outdoor activity due to high heat and humidity. The previous evening had been long and we were facing the sun most of the afternoon. Guys nodded off, including me.

Little Man hid in the woods with binoculars and wrote down the names of everyone who had their eyes closed. At the end of training, he formed us up and read off the names. If your name wasn't read, you were instructed to get on the trucks and the truck drivers were instructed to drive to the bowling alley parking lot out of sight of our Company area.

We miscreants ran two and a half miles, in "Red Flag" (90+ degrees and 90+ humidity) conditions, from the range to the bowling alley and boarded the waiting trucks for the last quarter mile to the Company area. As soon as we got in the barracks, guys started passing out. It quickly became apparent to the rest of the cadre that something was badly wrong. Ambulances shuttled 28 guys to the hospital emergency room. Head counts kept coming up short and search parties roamed the barracks looking for missing men. I was one of the last found. I was on the cool tile floor of one of the latrines wrapped around a toilet.

I was a desert boy and recovered quickly but 12 guys were kept at the hospital overnight and apparently one almost died. Another "how not to" learning experience. Little Man was immediately reassigned to a unit in Korea and the Inspector General opened an investigation into the incident.

Another lesson in bad leadership which I remember to this day.

III

Basic and Advanced Infantry training had turned out to be fun. I learned to play the game with the cadre and there were a few of us who liked to mess with the Drill Sergeants. If we got away with it, they admired us and in private moments they would acknowledge, "That was a good one.", but if they caught us we paid a price. One day while in OCS I did over 1300 pushups because I had sprayed "Pledge Wax" on our linoleum floor and the Tactical (TAC) Officer had come into our room and slipped and fell on his ass. It was worth it.

In OCS there were strict rules regarding contraband food (Pogy Bait) and many of us subverted the rules. Pizza delivery was especially fun. A whole Platoon would order Pizza delivery and request that the delivery man come to a place at the back where he was to place the pizzas in a garbage can which had been lowered from an upper floor by ropes. Up would go the pizzas and down would come the money. If the Duty Officer caught us a price was paid. I think the funniest one that happened to me was getting caught by a TAC Officer who had a great sense of humor. He extracted a couple of pieces for himself and then ordered us into the showers, turned on the water, and handed us the pizza boxes. He wished us good night with the admonition not to turn off the water until we finished our pizza. We didn't. That was part of the game.

The move I was most proud of was connected to my love of Wint-o-Green Life Savers. I was addicted to them and hid them in our two-man room. Of course you could smell them and the TAC Officers went nuts trying to find them. Several times they tossed my room like an experienced Narcs with a search warrant. Part of the game was that they wouldn't order me to turn them over. They had to find them and then they could rain on me to their hearts content. They never found the Life Savers.

At graduation, my TAC Officer, John Coughlin, accompanied by several other TAC Officers came up to me and shook my hand saying," We know you had Wintergreen candy in your room. Now that we are all officers will you tell us where you hid it?" Sure!

We had study lamps on our desks that had two short neon tubes for light. I had carefully removed the guts of the back tube and secreted my Life Savers in there. They were never discovered. They all shook my hand and gave me a well done. A glorious moment!

I think becoming an officer may have been a mistake on my part. Although I think I was a good officer and I thrived on the responsibilities, I might have been smarter to stay on the Special Forces medic course. Special Forces medics are among the best emergency medical practitioners in the world. As much as I loved the leadership role of being an officer, I think being a medic would have changed my life.

After attending Jump School, my first assignment was to the 3rd Special Forces Group (Airborne) for the purposes of attending Special Forces Officers' Training at Fort Bragg, North Carolina, "Home of the Airborne". One of the nice things about the Army was, no matter where you went you were always at somebody's "Home".

When I arrived at Ft. Bragg, I was allowed one week in the BOQ (Bachelor Officer Quarters), and then I had to find Off-Post housing. The guy in the next room was also there for Special Forces training so we spoke every evening. It took about two minutes to figure out that he was there to please his father who had been a paratrooper in World War II. He was a tragedy looking for a place to happen. He was slim to the point of frailty and I assumed he was also gay. My guess was he spent his whole life trying to live up to what he perceived his father's expectations to be and failed as often as not. Every time I spoke to him I would ask him if this was what he truly wanted to do and I would discuss alternatives. It wasn't what he wanted but he had to try for his father. He hung himself at the end of the week. It was sad and unnecessary.

I finally found an apartment which I shared with three other lieutenants, two of whom I didn't initially know. It was a three bedroom apartment. Doug Burdick, Toby Coyle, and I had bedrooms. Paul Zeh, who had been at OCS with me, slept on the couch and used the coat closet for his stuff. We called him "Piggy". He never did laundry. When his underwear or socks got so nasty he couldn't wear them anymore, he just threw them on the floor of the coat closet and bought more.

Several weeks after moving in, I left for about 6 weeks to go on a FTX (Field Training Exercise) in Utah and Montana. I was sure the jump in would be cancelled because of the weather. There were "blizzard" conditions forecast in the area of the drop zone, but somewhere near Camp Roberts, a National Guard Camp south of Salt Lake City, the Loadmaster retracted the door and snow came swirling into the C-130. The Jumpmaster signaled me into the door. I could barely see the ground because of wind driven snow, but several seconds later the jump light changed to green and I leapt into the storm. The plane was traveling over 100 miles per hour and fat, wet snowflakes pelted me in the face and they stung. For me it was a night jump because I had my eyes shut tight to keep the snow from blinding me. It generally takes about 3 seconds for the chaos accompanying the exit from the plane to settle down and then you enjoy a wonderful floating sensation for about 10 to 15 seconds before preparing to land.

We parachuted into a large, snow covered field south of Salt Lake City and landed in about two feet of snow. That was my first jump after "Jump School". It was called the "Cherry Jump". We rolled up our chutes and stuffed them in our kit bags and started for the turn-in point.

A State Highway ran by the fields we were using as a Drop Zone (DZ) and hundreds of people had come out to watch the jump. Some were co-eds from nearby colleges and universities. They all stayed in their cars with the heaters running. They would roll the windows down as we passed by. I collected several beers and slips of paper with phone numbers on them as I trudged head down through the blowing snow to the parachute turn-in point. I hadn't met any girls since leaving

Tucson, except for an Army nurse I took to the 18th Week Party during OCS. This was kind of encouraging, but I was really shy and I never called any of the numbers.

Most of the Group went to Park City, UT, to learn how to ski; as Assistant Operations Officer, I went to Mount Pleasant, UT, to set up a headquarters for the exercise. Rumor had it that life was pretty good in Park City. The 3rd Group guys stayed in motels and hit the slopes during the day and the bars at night. In Mount Pleasant we slept on cots in the National Guard Armory Gym. No slopes, no bars. Welcome to my world.

I did have a wonderful encounter with an old man whose name was Draper. While looking over the town's dirt airstrip as a possible Drop Zone for a bunch of us who wanted to make a parachute jump, the Team Commander and I were buzzed by a Piper Cub. The Cub circled and landed. The pilot, wearing denim overalls over a dirty flannel shirt, and sporting a grey beard and an old man's shuffle, introduced himself as Draper, just Draper, and asked what we were doing. I told him I was reconnoitering the area for a training exercise and thought the airstrip might make a good Drop Zone for a parachute jump. He informed me it was private property but since he was the owner, we could use it any time. Then he offered to take me on an aerial tour of the area. Heck yea!

I got in the little plane and we took off. We didn't get more than 50 feet up and Draper said he needed gas. Why didn't he get it before we took off? With that we landed on a long straight-a-way on Highway 89 and taxied to the edge of town where his gas station was. He got out and went to the nearest pump, came back to the plane dragging a long gas hose, put the nozzle in the tank and filled it up with High Test. While the tank was filling, Draper and I got to talking. I was informed that he bought the plane carcass as salvage and decided to rebuild it. It was not registered and he didn't have a pilot's license. He had taught himself to fly after "pranging the kite a few times." This was turning into a real adventure.

After waiting for a car to pass, we taxied back onto Highway 89 and took off, turning east toward the mountains. Draper stayed low, explaining that every time he went too high he came up on radar which on occasion resulted in visits from the government. He didn't like the government so it was better to stay low. I was loving it. What a character!

We started up a canyon and Draper spotted a herd of elk. He handed me a stainless steel derringer and said," give it a try." I didn't want to kill any elk but I figured a .22 or maybe a .22 Magnum derringer wasn't going to do much and the chances of hitting anything other than the ground were about zero. BLAM! I nearly dropped the gun and while I was juggling the gun back into the plane I was screaming, "WHAT THE HELL WAS THAT?"

".357 Magnum."

"Where the hell did you get a .357 Magnum Derringer", I asked?

"I made it", he said.

I was full of questions. It was obvious to me that Draper didn't take kindly to too many people but for some reason he took a liking to me and I visited with him at his shop as often as I could while I was there.

Custom knife making was Draper's passion and there were several other very good knife makers in the immediate area. His shop had a pieced together look and was built from whatever was available at the time...logs, boards, railroad ties, etc. The floor was covered in sawdust and the room was cluttered with saws, grinders, a forge, and other tools of his trade as well as antlers, exotic woods, and stainless steel rods of all diameters. It smelled of leather and wood smoke. We had a great talk and I learned a bit about knife making.

Draper was one of those fascinating old guys you meet on the back roads who are full of wisdom and idiosyncrasies and I enjoyed our time together. I regretted it when it was time to leave. Although I never saw Draper again, I did order one of his knives which I carried on my second tour in Vietnam.

There were some injuries during the ski training, including one to the Operations Officer for a team going to Montana. I was transferred to that team to be the replacement Operations Officer. Our method of infiltration was supposed to be a night jump into a small pasture outside Deer Lodge, MT, but we got delayed because of a blizzard. We spent the night on the cold, hard floor of a hangar at Hill Air Force Base.

We took off from Hill AFB in a C-123 the next morning a little after sunrise. The blizzard was gone and it was clear and cold. We "chuted up" enroute and about half an hour out from our drop area, the C-123 descended to about 200 feet and began "Nap of the Earth" flying to simulate penetration into enemy-held territory. I was glad I hadn't eaten any breakfast!

We arrived at our "Drop Zone", but of course nobody was there because the jump had been cancelled the night before. The DZ party that was supposed to set up the Zone had not gotten word that we were still coming. The decision was made to jump. The Jumpmaster picked out a likely DZ, and although we had no idea about ground conditions or wind speed and direction, we jumped.

The wind must have been about 25 knots! Twelve to eighteen knot winds were the upper limit in training. We exited the aircraft and after my chute opened I realized I was moving along at a pretty good clip. Fortunately, the cold air kept us aloft for a few extra seconds, giving me time to release my ruck sack which was secured to one end of a fifteen foot strap, and start a turn into the wind to slow down a bit.

I landed really hard. I think I blacked out for a few seconds. When I came to, I was being blown face down along an icy, muddy pasture. I rolled onto my back and tried to clear my canopy releases of ice and mud so I could detach my parachute and collapse it to end my unscheduled trip through what turned out to be a cow pasture. But before I succeeded, my parachute caught on a barbed wire fence and collapsed itself.

I had been blown about sixty yards, at least half the distance I was face down. I was covered in mud and had wet cow pies stacked from the top of my reserve chute to my chin. Both knees were ripped out of my fatigues and one of my boot laces was broken. To make matters worse, my rucksack had burst open and my belongings were scattered everywhere. My socks and underwear were blowing in the wind. I don't think I found everything I had packed in the short time I had to collect my things. Several jumpers sustained sprains and everyone was roughed up a little bit. We were lucky there were no serious injuries!

Somebody showed up with a couple of horses and we packed all our gear on them and began our march into the mountains. Our destination was an old silver mine several miles back in the hills. It was cold but not uncomfortably so. We reached the mine in an about two hours. Fortunately there was a cabin there that we could stay in.

For the next few weeks we attacked the Montana National Guard in brutally cold weather. Tough sledding for a desert boy. When the exercise ended, we boarded a C-123 at the Bozeman, Montana airport and headed back to Ft. Bragg. It took 14 hours to fly back. The C-123 is a very slow plane.

I started The Special Forces Officer Course at Ft. Bragg shortly after returning from the FTX. It was a fascinating curriculum. We studied lots of history and tactics relating to unconventional warfare and read about two books a week relating to Guerilla Warfare and the Viet Cong. We also learned to fire, disassemble, and reassemble almost every infantry weapon in the world. We could blow up a house without disturbing the neighbors, fashion makeshift explosives from everyday items, encrypt and decrypt messages and communications, run spy networks, call in airstrikes and set up drop zones, and a myriad of other skills.

The training culminated in a week long field exercise called "Robin Sage" at Camp McCall, an auxiliary air field and training area built during the Second World War. It was a great learning experience. The team I was on parachuted from a C-123 into a small corn field about 2 AM. It was the only time in 80 plus jumps that I missed the Drop Zone. I was slow to get oriented in the dark and I landed in a tree.

The power company had turned off the power in the area for about an hour during the jumps so nobody would be hurt if they hit a power line. Everything was blacked out except the yard/security lights in the farmyards. Those lights were on auxiliary power and remained on. Unfortunately several chicken farms were affected. Rumor was, when the lights went out in the chicken coops, the chickens panicked and ran to the ends of the coops where the security lights were and lots of chickens smothered. The Mess Halls at Ft. Bragg served chicken for the next three days.

"Robin Sage" was fun but challenging. Very little sleep and constant ambushes. It brought into play almost every aspect of our training and it really reinforced my confidence. I felt I knew what I was doing. At the end of the week we trucked back to Ft. Bragg and some much needed sleep.

Luckily for me, Doug Burdick, one of my roommates, had hooked up with a girl who worked at the hospital as a Med-tech. I got set up on a reluctant blind date with one of her hometown girlfriends for a weekend. She was coming to Ft. Bragg for the welcome home party celebrating our return from Utah and Montana.

I was standing on our second-floor balcony when Laura, Doug's girlfriend, drove up in his red convertible Corvette. The little blind date girl got out and made a great first impression. Blonde, nicely dressed, trim, the whole nine yards. Maybe a little bit too sorority looking but so far, so good.

She was a typical blind date. She didn't want to be there and acted like she was doing me a favor. Obviously she thought she was too good for me. She seemed very materialistic and didn't like the way I was dressed. I guess she was more into frat boys. She was pretty shallow and stuck-up in my opinion, but she was really cute! I began to fall in love immediately. By the end of the weekend she found me tolerable, so we saw each other again…and again.

For the next several months I made the trip from Fayetteville to Roanoke Rapids, North Carolina in my brand new Chevelle Super Sport almost every weekend. I spent the weekends in a small North Carolina town going to the movies and learning to like vegetables. I was a goner. I loved the little blind date girl. I would tell her I loved her and she would say, "Ditto." She just wouldn't say "I love you" back. Troubling, but not a deal breaker.

In the blink of an eye, it was time to leave for Vietnam. The little blind date girl came to Tucson to see me off and ease my mind about my future with her. I had a great time showing her around my part of the country. On one of the last nights of my leave we went to a steakhouse called the "Cork and Cleaver". We were enjoying the meal and the music when "Night and Day" by Sergio Mendez began playing. It became "our" song and turned the evening into one I will always remember.

The 30-day leave in Tucson ended quickly and in early September 1967, I boarded an American Airlines flight from Tucson to San Francisco on the first leg of my adventure. I was more than motivated to see what the conflict in Vietnam was all about but saying good-bye to the little blind date girl was one of the hardest things I've ever done.

My seatmate on the flight to San Francisco was an Air Force First Lieutenant who had just finished F-4 Pilot Training at Davis Monthan Air Force Base in Tucson. He was on his way to Thailand.

We hit it off right away. By the time we landed in San Francisco, we were good friends. Something about the specter of imminent combat and possible death intensifies relationships and I enjoyed talking to him during the flight. That being said, my seatmate and I did not exchange contact information and I do not remember his name. He was a good guy and I hope he made it home all right.

He said his sister was a stewardess (in those days they were not known as "Flight Attendants" and there were few, if any, males working anywhere but on the flight deck of the aircraft...it was a simpler time). She lived in San Francisco with a roommate whom he dated when he could. He showed me their pictures. Very attractive! He was going to stay at their apartment a few days. I could stay there too if I wished. He was sure it wouldn't be a problem. It sounded good to me! I was on my way to war, I was single and I was up for almost anything.

When we got to San Francisco, we shared a cab to his sister's apartment. He had a key, so we let ourselves in. It was a very nice two-bedroom apartment in a good neighborhood. This was going to be great! Things were definitely looking up until he spotted the note on the mantel over the fireplace.

It informed him that both girls had been called away for the week to work extra flights or something to that effect. He was to make himself at home and they would see him when he came through next year on his way home. They were really sorry to have missed him.

They weren't nearly as sorry as I was! Again, welcome to my world. On the other hand, thoughts of the little blind date girl filled my mind morning, noon, and night so it really didn't matter.

I was in love and although the little blind date girl would not consider engagement or possible marriage while the specter of Vietnam loomed in our immediate future; if I survived, I would ask her to marry me. It was the only bug on my windshield. I really wanted to go to war with no emotional encumbrances and although there was no formal declaration of future plans, I was very much committed to the relationship.

IV

I called in to the Replacement Depot in Oakland to find out when and where to report and was informed that my first flight to Vietnam was cancelled and I had to wait 3 extra days for my next assigned flight. I stayed the three days at the apartment belonging to the stewardesses courtesy of the F-4 pilot. When I left, I put the key and a Thank You Note in one of my berets and left it on the mantel where the note had been. I've often wondered what they must have thought and if they ever wondered what happened to their unknown houseguest.

I spent my time around San Francisco doing "touristy" things, as long as they were free. It was not a friendly town if you were in the military. You could put on civilian clothes, but the "high and tight" haircut wasn't going to fool anybody. It was a relatively lonely few days and I had little interaction with people. I did not leave my heart in San Francisco. As far as I was concerned, the people there were a bunch of jerks!

I was so broke there wasn't much I could do, so I stayed out of trouble. Besides, I was chomping at the bit to get going. I was trained and confident. I loved my country and trusted its people, politicians, and press. Despite that, I held no romantic illusions about combat. I knew my life would be forever changed by the coming experience and that there was a possibility that I might never again see the country and people I loved.

The three days passed quickly enough and I was soon boarding a United Airlines DC-8 bound for Cam Ranh Bay, Republic of South Vietnam. That was in the days before contract carriers like Flying Tiger or World Airways completely took over the movement of troops in aircraft configured like cattle cars. The DC-8 I was on was a real civilian airliner. Because I was an officer, I was seated in the First Class Cabin.

So there I was at 35,000 feet, sitting in First Class, and heading for Honolulu. The stewardesses had somehow managed to change into Hawaiian outfits and were handing out red terrycloth slippers so we could get comfortable and enjoy the Polynesian themed meal they were passing out on our flight to paradise. It was like a holiday.

Initially, I resisted the slippers. I was Airborne and a Special Forces Officer for Pete's sake. "Legs" (non-Airborne) wore shoes; I wore trousers bloused over highly shined jump boots. It was a point of pride…besides the boots were hard to take off in the confines of an airline seat. I noticed that the "legs" (non-airborne) were neither impressed, nor bothered, by my choice of footwear and I eventually succumbed to the red slippers and the luxury of being able to wiggle my toes. I still felt like I was going on holiday, but thoughts of the future and the unknown were creeping into my consciousness. My destiny awaited and I was speeding toward it wearing red terrycloth slippers. I liked the incongruity of it all.

The pitch of the big jet's engines eventually changed and we began to descend toward the

Hawaiian Islands for refueling and a crew change. It really did look like paradise. I saw ocean, beaches, lush greenery, beautiful hotels and people. Hawaii had all the accoutrements of an idyllic vacation spot. (Remember, I grew up in a desert and I was broke. It didn't take very much to impress me.) This was a lifestyle I could easily embrace. Maybe if I got back from Vietnam, I could visit as a real person. It did seem a little warm and humid though. Little did I know!

We were in Honolulu for a few hours and I got to see the airport terminal. Many hours later we repeated the process of fueling and crew change in the Philippines and I got to see all of Clark Air Force Base that you could see from the Transient Terminal. It seemed warmer and more humid than Hawaii. We re-boarded for our final destination and suddenly it was very real, very strange, and for me, very exciting!

We continued westward and at some point the pilot announced that we had two hours to go. I had a window seat and though it was premature, I began to strain for my first glimpse of "the Nam". It was Wednesday, September 13, 1967.

Once again, the pitch of the engines changed, and we started our descent. Finally I noted some discoloration on the horizon. It wasn't exactly hazy; it was more "smudgy". It made sense when you think about it; a normal coastal area is commonly wrapped in haze due to humidity and sometimes pollution. Vietnam had high humidity, but it was pollution on a whole new scale that caused it to be "smudgy".

Once you become accustomed to the environment of war, you realize that it really messes up the air quality, something is always burning…trees, structures, just about anything that is combustible…and bombs and artillery constantly churn the ground. It wraps the area, not in haze, but in smudge. All the junk in the air made for some beautiful sunsets though.

We landed at the Cam Ranh Bay Airbase. This was the war zone. Columns of smoke rose from the distant hills; fighters and transports took off every few minutes. Soldiers in various uniforms were everywhere. I was excited.

Two things immediately struck me upon my arrival in Vietnam from the "world". One was the climate! Despite the fact that I was arriving from a military base in the Southeastern United States where heat, humidity, and bugs had been on the daily training schedule, and I had gotten a taste of the Southeast Asian climate in Hawaii and the Philippines, nothing prepared me for the blast of hot wet air that hit me when I first stepped out of the airplane. It stunned me after many hours of air-conditioned comfort in the civilian airliner. I moved rather smartly to the air-conditioned bus, with wire mesh over the windows to deflect grenades, that would take me to in-processing while enduring catcalls from the soldiers and airmen who had finished their tours of duty and were waiting to board our "Freedom Bird" back to the "world".

The second thing for which I was not prepared was the odor. Most third world countries have an "exotic" odor that is usually a combination of raw sewage and local foods being prepared. The smell of Vietnam was a little different than anywhere else I had visited and is undoubtedly remembered by everyone who served there, whether they lived and slept in the jungle dirt or pounded typewriter keys in air-conditioned offices. Initially, it was cloyingly sweet, sickening, and constant in the built-up rear areas but eventually I got used to it.

The unique smell of Vietnam in the areas populated by the U.S. Military was undoubtedly due to the method used to dispose of human waste. In the villages, the local people pretty much "went" wherever the spirit moved them, frequently in the rice paddies or gardens, where excrement was used as fertilizer. It was different in the military locations.

Anyplace that was a secure military area without indoor plumbing, disposed of human waste by burning. The latrines (Army for toilets) consisted of small shacks with boards positioned over cut down 55-gallon drums containing several inches of diesel fuel. The boards had holes cut in them for the obvious purpose. Some of the boards even had toilet seats affixed to them for the soldier's added comfort. These latrines were augmented by "piss tubes"; rocket and artillery packing tubes sunk partway into the soil and filled with sand or gravel, into which a soldier could urinate.

The problem with urine pretty much took care of itself, but feces was another matter. In the heat and humidity of Vietnam, diseases, and more especially flies, were major problems. To counter these problems, waste disposal was a priority and occurred about every 12 to 24 hours. The task usually fell to a Vietnamese laborer and was accomplished by pulling the cut down drums full of waste from the back of the latrine, dragging them a safe distance, and setting them on fire. The drums were burned out until there was no residue left. Once they had cooled, they were refilled with diesel and replaced in the latrine.

Frequently "accidental disposal" occurred when a smoker would unconsciously drop a cigarette butt in the "toilet" after completing his "business". Ignition might not occur for hours. Several times during my two tours of duty "Chinese Fire Drills" that accompanied burning latrines awakened me in the middle of the night. There was no point in trying to extinguish the fire, so after the initial flurry of activity, we would all stand around and watch them burn. The end result was a little more smudge and a little more smell. It was just one of the many culture shocks that a new arrival had to overcome.

I don't have much recollection of my initial stay at Cam Ranh Bay. It was a huge logistical area that was getting bigger by the day as the United States Military built up forces in Vietnam. The Army area we were in was near the beach and all I remember was sand and the standard quarters that I would find in every rear area in Vietnam that I ever had the pleasure of visiting.

The sand was a dazzling off-white color and contrasted beautifully with the turquoise waters of the South China Sea. It was beautiful beyond description.

The buildings, on the other hand, were gray/brown and had wood floors and corrugated tin roofs. The lower halves of the walls were wood siding and the upper halves were screened to let in the breeze and keep out the bugs. In the Army and Marine areas, a three-foot high wall of sand bags surrounded the buildings, built to protect occupants from bullets and fragments in the event of attack. The Navy and Air Force areas were generally considered more secure and sand bags were not used very often.

We turned in all our U.S. money in exchange for Military Payment Certificates (MPC). MPC's were paper money in amounts of 5 cents, 10 cents, 25 cents, 50 cents, 1 dollar, 5 dollars, 10 dollars, and starting in 1968 20 dollars. It was illegal for unauthorized (read that as non-U.S.) personnel to possess MPC, and that policy, in theory, eliminated black market currency speculation. It was like Monopoly Money in size and colors and it got changed several times a year to deter black marketers and reduce hoarding, as the old style would become worthless. Conversion-days in Vietnam were always classified, never pre-announced. On C-day, soldiers would be restricted to base, preventing them from helping Vietnamese civilians convert old MPC to the newer version. Since Vietnamese were not allowed to convert the currency, they frequently lost savings by holding old, worthless MPC.

We also endured the obligatory medical review and lectures regarding the various and sundry tropical flora and fauna, as well as the venereal diseases that abounded in Vietnam, including the infamous "Black Syph" legend. I think every war in history has had the same legend regarding venereal disease...the strain that modern medicine can't cure, so if you get it you will be sent to an isolated island, never to see your loved ones again. There was an island off the Philippines, which was visited by at least 600 returning GI's who spent an average of 11 months there before they were cured and released to return home. I know it's true because my barber worked there and told me about it.

We "swished" mouths full of Fluoride and took our first weekly malaria tablets. I don't know how effective the big orange tablets were in protecting us against malaria, but as an antidote for constipation, they were unsurpassed. Then we were given our orders assigning us to the various units "in country".

Many soldiers had their orders changed due to "the needs of the service", but my orders assigning me to the 5th Special Forces Group (Abn) remained in force. I would have been inconsolable if, after all my preparation, I had been reassigned. The next morning a deuce and a half (2 ½ ton truck) showed up with a driver and a Sergeant First Class (SFC) wearing a Green Beret and carrying a .30 caliber carbine. He was most impressive and he said, "Everyone going to Fifth Group get in the truck." So I did.

I figured that we were going back to the airfield for a flight to Nha Trang, "Home of the 5th Special Forces Group", but it soon became apparent that we were leaving Cam Ranh Bay and heading north on the infamous Highway 1. Bernard Fall's book titled "Street without Joy" was named for Highway 1. The book detailed the destruction of the French Expeditionary

Corps at the hands of the Vietminh, the forerunners of the Viet Cong, during the French Indochina War. It had been required reading at the Special Warfare Center during my Special Forces Officer's Course. I knew Highway 1 was ambush alley!

Since we had not been issued weapons and there were no armored vehicles or gun jeeps escorting us, I began a rather earnest conversation with the formally impressive, now dangerously insane, SFC who was running this "goat rope". His lack of concern appalled me. According to him, it would take an hour, perhaps more, to get to Nha Trang on good old "Bloody One", but it was a secure area and there was no danger. Obviously this guy had not been watching the six o'clock news.

The conversation ended with him allowing me to carry his carbine for the remainder of the trip. If we were ambushed, at least I would go down fighting! I had a lot to learn.

The highway gradually left the coastal lowlands and entered some foothills of low limestone karsts. (Limestone formations with sheer, but pitted, sides that rose up from the valley floor. Caused by years of erosion, karsts are common in many parts of Southeast Asia). Once again, the beauty of the Vietnamese countryside struck me. It very much resembled the beautiful, stylized paintings that I had seen in Chinese and Japanese restaurants. The vegetation was lush and green and the scenery was breathtaking. Unfortunately, the vegetation grew right to the edge of the road. It was perfect ambush country. I felt as though we were being watched.

The highway wound through the small karsts and as we rounded one of the larger formations, we came upon a small military facility. Within the compound, a company of Republic of Korea Marines, wearing white Gis, engaged in Tae Kwon Do practice. I had heard about them and they certainly looked as tough as their reputation. Even at 250 yards they exuded an aura of lethality. They were warriors to a man. No wonder the SFC considered this area secure. I handed his carbine back to him and settled in to enjoy the rest of the ride while I tried to ignore his smirk. It was not the first or last time I would feel stupid as I "learned the ropes."

I arrived in Nha Trang and found it to be a beautiful, though somewhat abused, coastal city, situated on a picturesque bay. Then, as now, it was a popular seaside resort destination. The buildings and people fascinated me. Nha Trang was typical of most of the cities I saw in Vietnam. The dwellings and small shops in the outlying areas were mainly bamboo or wood frames covered with thick layers of rice thatch. As our deuce and a half traveled closer to the city, I saw much more corrugated metal used in the construction of shops and roadside stands. It was clear that many of the metal sheets were rejected from can companies because of incomplete logo printing. Some of the structures looked as though they had been made of flattened beer or soda cans. As we closed on the city proper, the architecture changed to mostly stucco buildings with red tile roofs. Most of the buildings were painted white or pastel colors.

In general, the Vietnamese people were small in stature. The people in the outlying areas were almost always involved with agriculture. Their dress was utilitarian…sandals, black pajama pants, lightweight, long sleeved tops, usually white or black, and conical straw hats. They looked old beyond their years. They generally traveled by foot or bicycle, unless they were traveling between towns in which case they took a bus. The buses were a sight to behold…overloaded and festooned with crates of chickens, pigs, and all manner of luggage. It seemed to me that the primary braking systems on the buses consisted of loud horns and shouting drivers…a lot like New York City taxis.

As I drew nearer to the city, modes of dress and transportation changed. Traffic consisted of thousands of bicycles, motor scooters, cyclos (a rickshaw like passenger compartment pushed or pulled by bicycles or motor scooters), and cars, almost all of which were low slung black Citroens similar to those I saw in "The Maltese Falcon" or news reels of Paris during the Second World War, and of course, Jeeps!

I saw men in more western garb…slacks, sport shirts, and even tropical suits. The majority of military-aged males were in uniform. The women almost always wore the Aou Dai, a beautiful form fitting silk high necked, ankle length dress, slit up the sides to the waist and worn over silk slacks. They reminded me of beautiful dolls because they were small in comparison to the girls I had known in the U.S.

We arrived at our destination around lunch time but we were not offered any chow. We had to wait until mid-afternoon to begin in-processing. Headquarters personnel, at least those involved with processing incoming troops, apparently observed the local custom of "Poc" time (Poc time, similar to Siesta, is a time honored tradition in warmer climates) and didn't return from lunch for several hours.

The 5th Special Forces Group (Abn) Headquarters was in a low white building with the ubiquitous corrugated tin roof, painted dark green. Flagpoles flanked the main entry with a large American Flag on the left and a large Republic of Vietnam Flag on the right. The rest of the construction in the headquarters compound was the usual wood/screened buildings with tin roofs. Other than the headquarters building, it looked like everywhere else.

I felt like a total outsider for the few days I was there and I don't remember much, other than I was treated as though I was a nuisance to the order and organization of the headquarters operation. It seemed as though they could hardly wait to be rid of me. To this day, I am resentful of the treatment I received at 5th Group Headquarters.

I found out I was to be part of the Special Operations Augmentation (SOA) theoretically under the operational control of MACV (Military Assistance Command Vietnam). I was specifically assigned to the Studies and Observation Group (SOG) and further assigned to CCN (Command and Control North) in Da Nang. I had no idea what they were talking about, but got the feeling that it was outside the mainstream mission of Special Forces, which might explain why I was getting such indifferent treatment at the hands of the 5th Special Forces Group personnel.

I recall that a lot of time was spent on processing a new Security Clearance. Assignment to SOG required a Top Secret Clearance and most of us arrived with lower level clearances. 5th Group would only be providing basic support and necessary paperwork functions and once I designated my next of kin, they had no further use for me. I pretty much got the "bum's rush" out of there and was on a very unusual C-130, heading for Da Nang the next morning.

The C-130 was undoubtedly used for more than transporting people and supplies around the country. It was painted flat black and dark green. The exterior of the aircraft was festooned with extra antennae and other special modifications. The covert nature of my assignment was becoming manifest. This was getting serious, but I was more excited than afraid. My adventure was beginning!

Arrival at Da Nang was a feast for my senses. I had always wanted to fly and knew I couldn't because I was color-blind. The disappointment did nothing to dull my love for aircraft.

Da Nang Air Base, the busiest airfield in the world at the time, was home to a montage of all types of Army, Air Force, Marine, Vietnamese Air Force (VNAF), CIA, and civilian aircraft imaginable, from the low and slow O-1 "Bird Dog" to the latest model of the

F-4 Phantom. It was noisy and smelled of jet exhaust. I loved it.

Little did I know that I would get more than my fair share of opportunities to fly in some of the planes I was seeing at the Da Nang Air Base. In addition, I would be witness to all sorts of demonstrations of skill and unbelievable courage on the part of pilots and crews of all the services and allied air forces involved in the effort to stop the spread of Communism. I am still in awe of the courage and competency of the aircrews that served in Southeast Asia. I am alive today because of them.

Another "Deuce and a Half", with another Sergeant First Class driving, awaited to take us to Command Control North (CCN) Headquarters in Da Nang. The CCN Headquarters compound was east, across the Han River (Song Han), on the South China Sea. On the drive over from the main airfield, we crossed the river, which was more like a sewer, and turned south down the beach road. We passed another, smaller airfield that was home to smaller (helicopters and bird-dogs) aircraft belonging to the Marines and Army. We turned into CCN/FOB 4 Headquarters just before reaching Marble Mountain, a black monolith sticking out of the sand. I was immediately struck by the very bad tactical location. To the south, Marble Mountain, looking directly down into the camp and a Vietnamese fishing village; to the west, a road, vegetation, and the Han River; to the north, a POW Camp for enemy prisoners; to the east, the ocean and the whole place was sort of haphazardly guarded by indigenous troops.

However, unlike Nha Trang, I was enthusiastically welcomed. I spent a day or two getting equipped and briefed. The briefings were thorough and I signed a document swearing not to reveal, in any way, what went on in SOG for twenty years following my assignment. I was also given a personal call sign: "Lancer". Everyone on the project had one. Theoretically they were picked at random from the Dictionary, but an awful lot of them seemed to fit the appearance or personality of the individual. I thought "Lancer" was pretty cool!

It was serious business. I found out I would be going further north to FOB 1 in Phu Bai.

The next morning before sunrise, I got my gear and went out to the helipad to board my ride north. And there were two of the sorriest excuses for helicopters I had ever seen! H-34's from the 219th "Kingbee" Squadron of the Vietnamese Air Force (VNAF). They were painted flat black and dark green with very light grey bottoms and no other markings. There was one WWII vintage .30 caliber machine gun in the cargo door of each chopper. The helicopters were filthy and covered with small pieces of aluminum pop riveted to their skin to cover up old bullet holes. To make matters worse, they were flown by Vietnamese air crews. I had not been warned and now I was sure I was going to die! Damn! This was starting to look like war!

During the next year I would come to love those beat-up old helicopters and I would be awestruck by the courage and abilities of the Vietnamese pilots who flew them, but at that moment I was speechless with disappointment. What kind of outfit was this? I thought we were supposed to have the best equipment available? We did…I just didn't recognize it at first!

The eastern sky was beginning to lighten and it was time to go. The pilots fired- up the big old birds. They had huge reciprocating engines in the nose. The pilot and co-pilot sat side by side above and slightly to the rear of the engine. Engine start was accomplished with a backfire or two and large clouds of blue/grey exhaust. The entire aircraft would oscillate for about 30 seconds and then everything would settle down to a dull roar.

Everything had been stripped from these old U. S. Army helicopters; they had no armor, minimal communications gear, one gun, and two pilots and a crew chief, who altogether wouldn't weigh 350 pounds. They were nimble. We didn't exactly take off the way helicopters did during my training. We leapt! I was beginning to realize that these were serious war machines and while their crews didn't worry much about going on parade, they did like to show off.

I settled in and watched the city of Da Nang wake up as we passed over. As we flew north along the Han River, I could see many winking lights as helicopters and light aircraft departed or maneuvered about the Marble Mountain airstrip. In the other direction, at the Da Nang Airbase, the "fast movers" were taking off for their assigned targets, afterburners glowing in the still dark sky. We flew north across Da Nang Bay, gaining altitude to clear Hai Van pass.

As the sun came up, Phu Bai Bay came into view. I was fascinated by the fish weirs, many of which seemed to be a hundred yards long. (Fish weirs are made with fencing which guide fish into traps) In a few moments we began a descent and followed good ole' "Bloody One" to Phu Bai. Highway 1 extended from the Delta to the DMZ along the eastern most portions of South Vietnam and just like the days of the French Indonesian War, was the scene of fierce and semi-constant combat.

FOB 1 was a forty-five minute chopper flight north of Da Nang and about ten kilometers south of the old Imperial City of Hue. The Headquarters of the 3rd Marine Division was at Phu Bai and there were various and sundry other units there as well. FOB 1, which had been a French Foreign Legion outpost at one time, was outside the Marine Division perimeter and was the northern most location of the Phu Bai military complex adjacent to Highway 1.

We had descended to about fifty feet as we flew over what would become my sometimes home for the next year. My address was LT. G. C. Dick, Drawer 22, APO San Francisco, CA...very clandestine. The "Kingbee" suddenly flipped on its right side, practically throwing me out the cargo door! We made a circle of the camp to make sure everyone knew we were coming, lined up on a large patch of oily dirt that already had several other "Kingbees" and two Marine Corps UH-1E gunships parked on it, flared and touched down, bounced slightly, and we were there.

There were faint sounds of artillery impacting and several columns of smoke rose from the hazy mountains to the west. A mixed group of Americans and indigenous soldiers were boarding two of the Kingbees and they looked badass. This was going to be shit-hot. I was a long way from the regular Army and I was a long way from Arizona and I was excited as I could be.

A three quarter ton truck, which was probably painted black under all the dirt and mud, was waiting to take our gear into the camp. All C and C vehicles were painted black and carried yellow Vietnamese license plates.

There were several other people reporting in with me, but I don't remember who they were. We checked in with the S-1 (Administrative Officer) and got our room assignments. FOB 1 had been an old French outpost, and there were several structures made of brick and plaster. Most of the original French outpost was to the south and was part of the Army of the Republic of Vietnam (ARVN...pronounced Arvin) Dong Da Training Center.

Before the day was over, I would meet a guy who would impact my life forever...1st Lieutenant William Oscar Vowel. He was my roommate, mentor, best man, and best friend for life. He was a big guy from Eight Mile, Alabama, and he had been the Army ROTC Drill Team Commander at the University of Alabama. He was Airborne-Ranger and he was "strack" (squared away). He was impressive and we fought some good fights together. He retired from the Army as a Colonel. He is one of my go to, life-long friends.

I dropped off my gear in Room #2. It was a four man room. Bill had the left rear spot and Alan "Chips" Fleming had the right rear spot. Chips is another lifelong friend. When I reported in, he was at "One Zero" school in Kham Duc. Chips' father was a Navy Admiral, but he only mentioned it once. He had been a Marine, before transferring to the Army and attending OCS. He retired from the Army Reserve as a Colonel.

I took the right front bunk. The left front remained empty, awaiting the next victim to be assigned to FOB 1.

I checked in with S-2 and S-3 (Intelligence and Operations), did some preliminary paperwork and met some people, then went to the S-4 (Logistics) to draw some equipment. I kept the M-16 that I had carried up from Da Nang and was issued an XM177E1 (we called it a CAR-15) sub-machinegun version of the M-16, and a Colt 1911 .45 caliber side-arm. A lot of guys badmouthed the M-16's. They had stoppages and misfires but I never had any trouble with my weapon. I took good care of it and it took good care of me. I loved that weapon.

I hung around for a week getting to know the place. Four things that were memorable the first week were the "Club", "Outgoing", the "Five AM Monkey", and "Padre" Baxter.

If the Tactical Operations Center (TOC) was the focal point of the daytime activities, then the Club was the nighttime focal point. Almost everyone went there after dinner for a drink or two or three. Drinks were 25 cents no matter what you ordered, as I recall. I drank mostly Coke. Lots of guys drank to excess and stayed until closing. I was generally in my room and writing my (almost) nightly letter to the little blind date girl by 2130 hours (9:30PM). Now that I was settled I could start receiving mail and sure enough there were already several letters from the little blind date girl waiting for me in the mail room. I was a happy man.

The first night I was there, I was awakened around 2300 hours by what sounded like loud explosions nearby. I bailed out of bed, grabbed my weapon and rushed outside thinking we were under attack. Someone saw me (I don't remember who), laughed, and told me it was outgoing artillery. A typical new guy mistake. It never occurred to me that we were close to any artillery, but the Third Marine Division was just down the road. Duh! Once I knew what it was, it never woke me up again.

The next morning, I was awakened by some awful screaming. It was still dark and the screaming was not human and not happy. It was the "Five AM Monkey". He belonged to the Club Sergeant. Apparently, sometime before I got there, several guys hatched a drunken plan to make the monkey Airborne qualified. He was fitted with a small parachute and taken up several hundred feet in a helicopter and released. The monkey didn't like the helicopter ride, but it really objected to the parachute drop. From that day forward he reacted quickly and loudly to the presence of nearby helicopters. His sensitivity to the sound of approaching helicopters was acute. When he was not in the Club Sergeant's room, he lived in one of the few trees on the FOB 1 compound. His favorite tree was outside Room #1. I lived in Room #2

Generally the choppers supporting FOB 1 arrived between 5 and 6 AM. The Five AM Monkey would hear them long before humans could and he would scream and run up and down the tree branches for many minutes at a time. Not good for those of us who were trying to catch some extra "Z's".

A lot of the indigenous troops terrorized the monkey by throwing sticks and stones at him. He had a good memory and when his terrorizers weren't paying attention, he would throw his poop at them. I felt sorry for him and would bring him fruit from the mess hall. He never bothered me. Sadly, he was killed during a rocket attack in February 1968.

My first Sunday morning at FOB 1 someone shook me awake…Master Sergeant Bruce Baxter. He said, "C'mon sir, it's time for church. I have a Deuce and a half waiting." I told him I didn't go to church, but I went to church that first Sunday. You don't refuse a respected Special Forces NCO, especially one of Baxter's stature. Several months later I would try to rescue Baxter and his Radio Operator, Joe Kusick, from a reconnaissance patrol that had major contact with the NVA southwest of Khe Sanh, but they had been killed before we got there.

Then it was off to One Zero School in Kham Duc. One Zero was the designation given to Recon Team Leaders. One was Assistant Team Leader, One

Two was the Radio Operator and One Three was anybody else (known as straphangers). The school covered general operating procedures as well as things that were unique to SOG.

To get there, I boarded a C-130 "Blackbird" bound for Da Nang. I spent the night at CCN and the next morning departed for Kham Duc in a "Kingbee". Kham Duc was southwest of Da Nang and about 15 kilometers from Laos. It was really wild country and the area between Da Nang and Kham Duc could only be described as "trackless jungle". The flight was…interesting.

As we lifted off from CCN, the Door Gunner/Crew Chief opened a new can of .30 caliber ammunition. Unfortunately, it was clipped for use in an M-1 and not belted for the machine gun. Useless! There was a belt with about 30 rounds of dirty, greasy ammo in the corner under the gunner's seat. He wiped it off with a dirty rag, loaded it in the gun, and gave me a "thumbs up" and an embarrassed grin, showing off his new gold tooth. A lot of the indigenous troops sported prominent gold dental work. I think it was like a savings account they could take with them. Great!

I then pointed out the transmission fluid that was steadily dripping from the overhead into a #10 Can on the floor. He gave me a "thumbs up" and a "toothy" grin. About thirty minutes later I tapped him on the shoulder again and pointed to the can which was now full. He radioed to the pilot over the intercom and gave me a "thumbs up" and another "toothy" grin…and we started to descend into a small jungle clearing.

There were four of us on-board the Kingbee and when it landed in the middle of nowhere we jumped out and took up security positions around the chopper. I looked back and watched, with some trepidation, as the crew chief climbed to the top of the H-34 with the coffee can of transmission fluid and dumped the contents of the can back into the transmission reservoir. All the while the rotor blades were turning at high idle just inches from his head.

We got back in quickly and lifted off and flew for another fifteen or twenty minutes before Kham Duc came into sight.

Kham Duc was definitely a frontier outpost. It was wild and beautiful country. The original 6000 foot runway had been built in the 1950's to bring in construction material to build a hunting lodge for Ngo Dinh Diem, the Vietnamese leader at the time. As far as I could tell, the lodge was gone and in its place was a Special Forces (SF) Camp. It was staffed by a Special Forces "A" Team, several companies of Montagnard troops and their families, the One Zero School Cadre and students, and sometimes some Air Force and/or Army Artillery folks.

This Camp was fairly typical of the Special Forces camps in South Vietnam. Militarily, South Vietnam was divided into 4 Corps areas. Each Corps had a number of SF Camps (generally in the far reaches of the Corps area, near the Cambodian and Laotian borders). The camps were staffed by 12 man "A" Teams, comprised of a Team Leader (CPT), Executive Officer (LT), Team/Operations NCO (MSG), Intelligence NCO (SFC), Weapons NCO (SFC), Assistant Weapons NCO (SSG), Engineer/Demolitions

NCO (SFC), Assistant Demo NCO (SSG), Communications NCO (SFC), Assistant Commo NCO (SSG), Team Medic (SFC), Assistant Team Medic (SSG).

The "A" Teams, or Operational Detachment A's (ODA), would recruit, equip, train, and lead local mercenary troops, similar to the way we did it in SOG. The mercenaries were paid by the U.S. and were called the Civilian Irregular Defense Group (CIDG). There was usually a Vietnamese Special Forces Team, called the Luc Luong Dac Biet, or LLDB for short, co-located with the U.S. Team. We remembered the official title by calling them the Look Long Duck Back. In many camps they did not participate in the monitoring and patrolling, but did participate vigorously in the black market and various medal ceremonies.

The SF/CIDG mission was to monitor the borders with Laos and Cambodia. Most of the troops were Montagnards, the mountain tribal peoples of Vietnam. Although they were considered to be inferior by the Vietnamese, they proved to be tough, courageous troops. Unlike the SOG mercenaries, their families lived in the SF camps with them. They were good soldiers and intensely loyal to the SF troops.

At Kham Duc, the camp was on the east side of the runway and a small village was on the west side. There were mountains all around. One of the big problems for the A Camps was that they had to be located by a runway and near water, so they were almost always on valley floors rather than hilltops. Tactically, the camps were at a real disadvantage when it came to terrain. The camps were frequently targeted by the NVA and were sometimes overrun. Kham Duc was attacked and overrun in May 1968.

A large hill was across the runway from the Kham Duc SF Camp and was manned by a small contingent of CIDG. The Republic of Viet Nam flag waved from the hilltop. They had a commanding view of the immediate area from there. The runway was challenging for pilots of fixed wing aircraft. There were some significant hills at one end and a cliff that dropped down to a river at the other.

Beyond the camp, the hills gave way to serious mountains with true triple-canopy jungle. The area was a beautiful rain forest full of deadly dangers. This wasn't so much like playing "Hide and Seek" anymore.

The usual One Zero Course was two weeks long and included a lot of training specific to running SOG reconnaissance patrols and concluded with a real patrol in the second week. During the first week we awoke early each morning and went for a run around the runway which I didn't like. Then we had some breakfast, which was usually good, and attended classes. A lot of the information was on communication. My second week was a little different in that SOG had just received some sensors known as PSID's (Patrol, Seismic Intrusion Devices) and we spent most of the second week experimenting with them.

The Signal Operating Instructions (SOI) developed for the patrols going into Laos were pretty clever in my opinion. They were one time use only and specific to the particular mission. I particularly remember the "Whisper code" which was used in close proximity to the enemy. It consisted of squelch breaks. Squelch is a break in static caused by holding down the push to talk switch on the radio and not saying anything.

We learned there was an Airborne Command Post that orbited in the area and when there were teams in the field, they would check on them if there was no Covey over the team. Call-signs were "Hillsboro" during the day and "Alley Cat" or "Moonbeam" at night. They could communicate directly with ground teams and relay information back to the various FOBs. In addition, there was an Army Mohawk (OV-1) Unit at Phu Bai that flew the trail at night taking photos and looking for trucks with Side-looking Airborne Radar (SLAR). Their call-sign was "Iron Spud" and they were very good about checking in on us at night.

There was also a totally random grid for secure communication. For example:

	67	12	93	48	55
Sport coat	Have sighted enemy	Contact immanent	Found 1 facility 2 truck park 3 supplies	Destroyed 1 facility 2 truck park 3 supplies	Need extraction
Bracelet	Need resupply	Have KIA #	Have WIA #	Have POW	Have Intel material
Slacks	Crossing stream	Found trail/road	Found comwire	RON	Need support

You might transmit Slacks 12 break Sport Coat 67 break Sport Coat 12 to let the FOB know you are about to spring an ambush. Anyone listening (and the NVA had much better monitoring capability than we originally thought) would not know for sure what you were saying. Once we were in contact we talked in the clear.

The second week, we headed out into the jungle to test the PSID's. The sets consisted of a base station which could be monitored by a patrol member using a headset and three remote Geophones with transmitters. They were spikes that were pushed into the ground and camouflaged. The range on the sets was limited, but they could be placed along a trail or around your perimeter at night to signal the enemy's approach. They reacted to seismic vibrations and alerted the operator to movement of people or larger animals…and there were lots of NVA and large animals in the area. One night we heard a big cat growling near the camp. The A Team guys said it was probably a tiger!

The first time we started down a small trail outside the camp, we were practicing moving silently as possible through heavy leaves. I decide that if the normal walking pace of a man was three miles per hour then a man might be able to move silently through dried leaves if he altered his pace to three hours per mile. We were going to go about a kilometer down the trail and set up an ambush to practice with the sensors. We'd gone about a hundred meters when the point-man froze.

The trail was alive! About a yard in front of the point-man the leaves on the trail started moving…a lot. At first we thought it was some kind of weird booby-trap or something. We carefully started brushing the leaves aside. Every time we moved, more of the trail was set into motion.

Dry forest leeches!! They sensed the approach of warm-blooded beings and would rise up trying to attach themselves so they could suck the blood of passing prey. There must have been hundreds of thousands of them! The leaves came alive for hundreds of yards!

We quickly learned to roll down our sleeves, button up our collars and soak any potential entry point (especially our flies) and any exposed skin in insect repellant and still they found ways to get to our skin and suck our blood. I never experienced leeches like that anywhere else on earth. They would start out about the size of a piece of macaroni, but after they sucked your blood they would be bigger than your thumb. We couldn't completely avoid them, so we concentrated on preventing as many as possible from attaching themselves to us. Very unpleasant business and some guys got some leeches in some really uncomfortable places. We got the leeches to release by burning them with lit cigarettes or dripping insect repellent on them.

We detached leeches and played with the PSID's for the rest of the second week and they were useful, but I never had occasion to use them on a real mission. Unbeknownst to me I was picking up lots of information about survival, reconnaissance, concealment, and a whole lot of other things that would help keep me alive. I no longer looked at the jungle, I looked into it. I didn't pay as much attention to the foliage as I did to the shadows. Seemingly little things, but they meant a lot. The week fairly flew by and we were on our way back to FOB 1 grateful for what we learned but wishing we could have spent a lot more time with the very experienced instructors.

When I got back from Kham Duc I began training with the Cambodian "Red Devils", a "battalion" made up of ethnic Cambodians living in Vietnam near the Seven Mountain Region manned the other, which was known as the "Red Devil Battalion". They were KKK (Khymer Kompuchea Krom) Cambodians. When they weren't fighting each other or the Viet Cong, I think they were bandits. They definitely knew how to employ the weapons we gave them.

Bill Vowell and I were the officers and a Temporary Duty (TDY) A Team from the 1st Special Forces Group in Okinawa, supplied the NCO Cadre. LT. Rod Hoepner, the Executive Officer of the TDY Team, joined us as an Officer on the Hatchet Force.

The A-Team from Okinawa, Team A-323, which trained and led (we were not Advisors) the Red Devils, was, from my perspective, one of the best in Special Forces. Master Sergeant Lloyd Fisher was the Team Sergeant.

Lloyd Fisher was a quiet, but forceful man. When he spoke, which wasn't often, you listened and obeyed. I never heard him raise his voice, even in heavy combat. Even though I had only been around him for a few weeks, he had my utmost respect and undivided attention, and it was more than obvious that his entire team felt the same way. His calming influence could never be dismissed. If I had to name the ten most influential people in my life, he would be high on the list.

Sergeant First Class Bruce Luttrell was the Team's Intelligence Sergeant. Bruce was high strung, but possessed a brave heart and was always where he was needed most. He saw humor in the world around him and I enjoyed being in his company. Regrettably, Bruce was killed on his second tour in Vietnam while serving with one of the 5th Special Forces Group's MIKE Forces (Mobile Strike Force).

One of the Team's Weapons Sergeants, SFC Earl Kalani, was already gone from Phu Bai. He was wounded in an exchange of gunfire with a VC who was about to shoot Bill Vowell in the back during a local operation. It happened before I got to FOB 1. Bill told me he owed his life to Earl. Sadly, Earl would die years later of complications during surgery to further repair the wound he received in that engagement. The other Weapons Sergeant was SFC Brooke Bell. He was quiet and competent. I didn't know him well because he tended to avoid officers. He did his job so well he rarely came to my attention.

The Demolitions Sergeants on Team A-323 were SFC Erskine "Ozzy" Osborne and SP5 Ulrich "Rick" Bayer. I hardly had a chance to get to know Sergeant Osborne. Within a few weeks he was wounded and would be evacuated from a hillside in Laos with a serious wound to his foot and lower leg. Rick Bayer was a bit of a wild one. He was an "adventurer" and was always involved in one scheme or another. I think "Top" Fisher did his best to hide Rick from me.

SFC Hamilton, or "Hambone" to his friends, was one of the Team's Communications Sergeants and was hard to overlook. He was a warrior. He was brave and aggressive to a fault. I admired him. He, on the other hand, didn't have much use for officers. He grudgingly tolerated me and that was enough. He would die of wounds received while saving the lives of the rest of the team, including mine, on a grassy plain in Laos early in 1968. It broke my heart and not a day goes by that I don't think about him and SGT. Gary Spann, a replacement for Kalani, who was also grievously wounded that day.

The Medics for the Team were Sergeant Ronald Bock and Sergeant First Class Jim Scurry. Jim was a bear of a man, but I never saw anyone as tender as he was treating the wounded or tending to the sick. He was also fearless and intelligent and was respected and admired by everyone. I was as in awe of him as I was MSG. Fisher and SFC. Hamilton.

Sergeant Bock was a fine medic and a very brave man, yet you got the idea that he wouldn't hurt a fly. He was tall and quiet. His studious nature reminded me of a college professor. I could easily picture him in a tweed sport coat with leather patches on the sleeves. He gave great consideration to everything he said. I don't know of anyone who didn't like him. I wrote him up for a Silver Star, for, among other things, using his body to shield wounded Cambodian soldiers from a mortar barrage. The fact that the SOG "culture" at the time, at least at FOB 1, did not award medals for bravery to members on missions "across the fence" who were not killed, should make his medal all the more significant.

Sergeant Phil Quinn was the Team's other Communications Sergeant. He had been assigned to the Radio Room in the TOC and would support us from Phu Bai.

We began training the "Red Devils" just to the west of camp in an area called Range 26. There was very little vegetation. I think it had been defoliated, not with Agent Orange but by the generations that preceded us in the area who cut the forest back for farming, cooking, and heating purposes.

It was obvious that our Cambodian soldiers knew their way around weapons. One day, the Cambodians, who loved to gamble, set up ammo boxes at 50, 100, 150, and 200 meters and began to take bets on their best "Thump Gunner's" ability (we called the M-79 Grenade Launcher a Thump Gun because of the sound it made). He had 4 grenades in the air before the first one hit and he hit every ammo box with direct hits. Impressive!

Another time, they wanted to bet that I couldn't hit a rock on the hillside about 25 meters away as many times as their best shot. I didn't take the bet, but I fired a magazine on semi-auto at the rock as fast as I could pull the trigger. Eighteen out of 18. Their guy missed twice. I should have taken the bet!

We never trained at night. Range 26 was a free-fire zone during the hours of darkness. We did, however, schedule night patrols in the "pacified area" northeast of camp. For our first patrol, we had intelligence that a Viet Cong tax collection party had been visiting the villages between Phu Bai and Hue. We were going to try and ambush them. Patrols like this were not part of our assigned mission, but we saw them as good training opportunities.

We left camp in some Deuce and a Halfs driven by U.S. Marines and headed north on Highway 1. We unloaded in a village south of the Perfume River and started across the rice paddies toward a bombed out village on a canal about a kilometer and a half to the east. As soon as the last man left the village, three shots came from the area we had just left. They were answered by three shots in the direction we were heading. So much for stealth and secrecy.

The Marines considered this a "Pacified" area…but they didn't come out here at night much. Many of our Recon teams (we called them "Spike Teams") had significant contacts in this area while on "training patrols".

We were wending our way along the paddy dikes and every now and then someone would slip and fall into the paddies which were filled with water from the recent early monsoon rains. There would be muttered curses in Cambodian, a splash, and then giggling. We would dutifully "shush" them. Then it was my turn.

I slipped, cursed, and fell backward into the paddy. Big splash! My rucksack, which contained a PRC-25 Radio, an extra radio battery, a couple of Claymore mines, some hand grenades, a bandolier of

40 Millimeter grenades for the M-79 Bill was carrying, a gallon of water, and a poncho liner, quickly filled up with water. I was doing a great imitation of a turtle on its back. I couldn't get up and I couldn't roll over. I heard giggling but nobody stopped to help me.

Finally one of the Cambodes at the end of the column extended his rifle to me and the two of us were able to get me out. But the column hadn't stopped and it was really dark. I couldn't see much of anything, but we started to double-time to catch up hoping we didn't miss any turns. A short while later I heard multiple safeties being clicked off. Fortunately we linked up without being shot.

We moved into the ambush site along a wide trail adjacent to a good sized canal that was overgrown with grass and weeds. The carcasses of bombed out and knocked down houses surrounded us. Most had stucco walls and had been painted white at one time. They were downright ghostly on this moonless night. Add to it a ground fog that hovered in the area and the whole scene was worthy of any Hollywood director's idea of a "bad things are about to happen" place. Spooky! It was about 2300 hours.

It wasn't long before one of the Cambodes began to cough like he had tuberculosis or something. The Medic, I think it might have been Jim Scurry, crawled over to him and gave him a big slug of cough syrup with codeine. Within the hour he was coughing again…more codeine. It wasn't long before he was at it again. Only this time about a half dozen of them were coughing. They had figured out that they could get free narcotics this way. Any hope of springing a successful ambush was gone thanks to the poor noise discipline. Jim finally ran out of cough syrup, but it was much too late to recover from the noise that had been made.

In the morning we packed up our stuff and headed back to the trucks. Our coughing Cambodes were so hammered one of them had to be carried. Their performance was an embarrassment to the Cambodian commanders and how they dealt with it, I don't know, but it didn't happen again.

I continued to learn valuable lessons and the number one lesson I learned from that debacle was...don't wear underwear. My shorts had been soaked with nasty, gritty paddy water and they wadded up and chaffed me raw. I was in real pain by the time we got back to camp. I'm surprised I didn't get some sort of deadly infection from that experience. "If you're going to be a commando, you might as well go commando" became my motto.

The other lesson was...lighten your load. If you know you'll need it, take it! If you're not sure you'll need it, leave it! I spent two years in Vietnam trying to figure out ways to carry less. Sometimes I wished I had something I'd left behind, but the critical items were: a little food, a lot of water, and extra radio batteries. Ammo, grenades, and a Claymore Mine were also must haves. Ponchos and liners were nice to have, so was an entrenching tool sometimes. I tried carrying a machete and White Phosphorous grenades...never needed them. After my first mission "across the fence" I began carrying a Bolo Knife. It was smaller than a machete, but would still cut trees. I always carried a signal mirror and a neon red and orange panel. I also had a piece of panel sown into the inside of my "boonie hat". If I ever lost all communication, I could turn my hat inside out and be seen from the air.

V

I had been back at Phu Bai for four days after my mission with the Nungs. Bill was still in Saigon being debriefed on that, our first mission. I was looking forward to Bill's return and a few weeks of preparation for the next mission, but stuff happens.

"Get that light out of my eyes! What the heck is wrong with you?"

"Sorry Lieutenant, they sent me over to wake you. They want you in the TOC (Tactical Operations Center) in fifteen minutes."

I had been back at camp four days. Bill was still in Saigon being debriefed. I knew that an unplanned early morning wake up was extremely unusual. "What's happening?", I asked.

"Baxter's team was hit hard, couple of choppers down, and Baxter, Kusick and some Air Force guys are unaccounted for. Covey has a beeper but no voice contact and they want your 'Hatchet Force' to go in and check it out," said the voice behind the flashlight. These types of Search and Rescue missions were known as "Bright Light" missions.

"Ok, I'm up. Have "Top" Fisher meet me at the TOC." I turned on my desk lamp and laced up my boots (we slept mostly clothed, even in camp, for obvious reasons).

Usually teams were given several weeks between missions to repack, and prepare for the next mission, so I knew that being sent back "across the fence" with little or no preparation time was unusual. I had a bad feeling about this!

Thankfully, I had cleaned my weapon, refilled my magazines, and already repacked my rucksack except for last minute items…food, water, and radio with extra batteries. My "ruck" probably weighed between 75 and 80 pounds when fully packed. My harness (belt and suspenders) probably weighed another thirty pounds. I wore almost all my ammo and two pints of water around my waist so that I would always have immediate access to it. Water and ammunition were precious commodities in "Indian Country."

We carried our magazines in canteen pouches because we could fit seven "mags" in a canteen pouch as opposed to four "mags" in a magazine pouch. I carried eighteen rounds to a magazine. Although a magazine could hold twenty rounds, the experienced men cautioned against filling a magazine all the way because it could weaken the magazine spring over time and cause a miss-feed.

I carried five pouches of magazines giving me a total of 649 rounds counting the magazine in my CAR-15 (a sub-machine gun version of the M-16) and a round in the chamber. That was a lot, but if I got into real trouble, which was what Hatchet Forces were there for, no one was going to loan me any ammo. Two pouches were filled with magazines that had sixteen rounds of ball ammo and two rounds of tracer at the bottom. The tracers alerted me to change magazines. These pouches were intended for use in a "last ditch effort"; because by the time I began using magazines from them, ammo would be a critical issue. One of my magazines was loaded with all tracers. They were useful in marking targets or showing friendly locations to pilots providing air support.

When the Hatchet Force went to the field, the commander carried the team radio and that added considerable weight to the rucksack. In most units, the leaders had RTO's (Radio/Telephone Operators) who carried the radio for them. With a large force of indigenous troops and only one or two interpreters, that was too much of a luxury. The other Special Forces Soldiers had their hands full without having one of them tied to the Commander because of the radio. We didn't consider having an indigenous RTO because of language difficulties. The radio was our lifeline and we didn't want out of our control.

Before leaving my room, I looked over at the empty bunks in the room. The one across from me at the front of the four-man room was currently empty and awaiting the next lieutenant assigned to FOB 1. The two areas at the back of the room were also empty, but for different reasons.

Diagonally across from my bunk was Bill's space. The other space at the back of the room belonged to 1LT. "Chips" Fleming. He was out on his first mission and was Assistant Team Leader to Master Sergeant (MSG) Bruce Baxter's Recon Team Utah.

Team Utah using the call sign "Flat Foot" was in trouble.

I knew "Chips" was with "Flat Foot" and I sent a quick, silent, prayer to the powers that be to take care of him until I could get there. Unknown to me at the time, he, and Staff Sergeant (SSG) Homer Wilson, the One-Three, were already at Phu Bai Med. They had been extracted by Spartan 52, one of the Hueys that had not been shot down during the exfiltration.

I hated the idea of going in harm's way without Bill Vowell, but I took comfort in knowing that the NCO's (Noncommissioned Officers, Sergeants and above) with whom I worked were the absolute best in the business.

In the early days of Special Forces, the Officers Corp of the United States Army considered a Special Forces assignment to be a dead end. Army Officers were well schooled in Cold War tactics. They were fully prepared to fight delaying actions in the Fulda Gap against the Russian and Eastern Bloc hoards, but little attention had been given to unconventional warfare. The traditional Corps and Division Officers were oriented toward conventional warfare and were not enthusiastic about embracing unconventional warfare training and doctrine...and they distrusted elite units. President Kennedy forced Special Forces upon them and they resented it.

Consequently, while led at the very top by unbelievably talented and visionary colonels and generals left over from WWII and the OSS, by and large, the majors and senior captains assigned to

Special Forces tended to be those who were left over after the conventional units had been staffed.

It was the opposite in the Noncommissioned ranks. Special Forces Units worldwide were blessed with the very best NCO's in the Army and there were no positions for inexperienced or junior enlisted personnel. Behind the scenes, the "Sergeant Majors' Mafia" ran Special Forces. Consequently, some NCO's looked at their officers with disdain.

That being said, I'd like to think of Lieutenants like Bill Vowell, Chips Fleming, myself, and others, as a new breed. Young, fresh, patriotic, aggressive, and smart enough to listen to our NCO's, performing in the field with dedication and professionalism, and bringing the teams back to camp with minimum casualties and missions accomplished.

The way SOG was set up; the NCO's were in charge of most field operations. Most of the officers assigned to SOG were staff officers. The few officers in SOG who were assigned to units that actually went into combat took their assignments and responsibilities very seriously. The smart officers took wise counsel from their NCO's. The not so smart commanders didn't last long. There was surprisingly little conflict. We were all professionals.

Word had traveled through camp just after dinner that "Flat Foot", had had contact with enemy trackers. That was bad, but didn't cause any immediate worry because it wasn't that unusual. Historically, NVA and Pathet Lao troops in Laos had not pursued Recon Teams in the dark. Generally Teams could break contact in the darkness and either continue their mission or make it to a cold (safe) PZ (Pick up zone) for extraction the next morning. There was another team in the area with "Flat Foot", using the call sign "Happy Times", and they went to ground and remained undetected.

I had checked in at the TOC early in the evening to see if everything was OK with the teams and was told that there was nothing unusual going on. I went back to my room to write my nightly letter to my unofficial fiancée and hit the rack (When I knew we were going out, I would post date letters to her so she wouldn't worry). Sometime during the night the situation radically changed for "Flat Foot".

I finished dressing, splashed some canteen water on my face and walked out to the piss tube to take a leak before going to the TOC. I felt gritty, but there would be no soap and water, no deodorant or shaving lotion, and no toothpaste if I were going into the field. Unnatural odors were to be avoided at all costs. Odors gave away the presence of others in an area. One of the problems we always had to contend with was the basic diet of fish verses a basic diet of beef. The different diets caused detectable differences in body odor in the field and frequently signaled the close proximity of the enemy. At least with a force the size of a Hatchet Force, we had enough indigenous troops to mask our "beefy" odor. Although it was a problem, I didn't know anybody who was willing to give up a steak in favor of a can of tuna. (Actually, salmon processed in Hong Kong was a mainstay of the NVA diet…the empty cans were frequently used in the construction of simple booby-traps).

I noticed that there was a lot of activity in the camp for 0400 (4:00 AM) as I headed over to the TOC.

Our TOC was a fairly large room with a briefing area that was about 30 feet long and 20 feet wide. The whole room was paneled in plywood that had been "Dog robbed" (acquired) through various trades with the Seabees and the Air Force. (They were suckers for fake NVA flags sprinkled with chicken blood and burned with cigarettes). A red curtain with the words, "TOP SECRET" on it, covered the north end of the TOC. There was a small podium in front of the curtain.

When I got to the TOC, there was standing room only. Marine aircrews from HMM-263 occupied most of the two-dozen or so folding chairs. HMM-263 had been moved from Chu Lai to Phu Bai several weeks before. They were not yet familiar with their new AO (Area of Operations) and had never supported one of our operations. As far as I knew, there had never been a briefing of all aircrews in our TOC. Usually the Flight Leads would get their briefing and go back to their helicopters, or to the club, and brief their people. My bad feeling just kept getting worse.

I had a quick word with MSG. Lloyd Fisher and asked him to get his team and the "Red Devil Battalion" ready. Naturally, he had already done that. He and his team were some of the most outstanding soldiers I had ever met, and the Red Devils were being readied for their first cross-border mission even as I mentioned it.

In reality, the Red Devils were not a battalion at all. On a good day they were a three-platoon company of Cambodian mercenaries. For this mission, they would number about 75. There would be twelve U.S. Special Forces personnel accompanying them.

I grabbed a bit of open wall next to another, much smaller red/TOP SECRET curtain. Behind that curtain was an 8x10 photo of a rather winsome lass in all her naked glory. Rumor was that she had been engaged to a member of one of the "Okinawa" teams at our camp, and had sent him a "Dear John" letter after he had been here several months, explaining that she had met a pilot who could offer her all the same things our guy had to offer, but with the added benefit of being with her rather than in Vietnam. She hoped he wouldn't mind if she kept the engagement ring as a memento of their time together and would he send back the picture of her that she let him take as a going away present?

He sent the picture back but kept the negative. He had the picture reprinted and, according to some, he had several thousand leaflets made up with the picture and her address which were dropped around some pretty remote firebases between Phu Bai and the Laotian Border. Supposedly she got a lot of unwanted mail, including a letter from an NVA soldier who happened upon one of the leaflets. No doubt the revenge was sweet, although returning to Okinawa while she was still there was out of the question.

Everyone settled down and Major (soon to be LTC.) Ira Snell, the camp Commander, came through the door from the radio room. Major Snell was an imposing figure to say the least. He had played college football and he was big and in shape. His jaw was like a hunk of granite and the madder he got the more he thrust it out. He was damn sure leading with his jaw this morning and looked like a battleship churning through the North Atlantic as he strode to the podium. My bad feeling just kept getting worse.

He stepped behind the podium and practically crushed it with hands that looked like black bear paws. A blood vessel pulsed in his dark forehead. He was tense! And then he began growling at the Marine aviators. "Everything you see, hear, smell, touch, or taste here, and that includes the coffee, is classified TOP SECRET. Nothing you learn here is to be shared with anyone outside this room. Does everyone understand that? Any breach of security will be dealt with quickly and severely. Everybody OK with that? Anybody wants to leave, leave now and nothing will ever be said. Does everyone understand?"

During a dramatic pause there were murmurs of assent and a lot of nervous looks. Naturally, no one left the room.

After a moment, Major Snell drew back the big red curtain revealing a large map of the northern portion of South Vietnam, the Demilitarized Zone (DMZ), the southern portion of North Vietnam, and the eastern portion of Laos. There were more murmurs and more nervous looks…and then the briefing began and my bad feeling just kept getting worse!

"The Camp you are in now is a part of SOG. SOG does not stand for Special Operations Group, as many people believe. It stands for Studies and Observation Group. Our mission is to do what we are told to do and part of that mission is to watch the Ho Chi Minh Trail and rescue downed pilots. That's why you're here this morning."

"Over the past few months, Intelligence has detected an escalation of NVA forces coming down the Trail. Recently we were tasked to monitor Route B-45 through what we know as Base Area 611. B-45 is a series of east-west connector trails between a main north-south corridor (Route 922) of the Ho Chi Minh Trail and the Ashau Valley."

"Yesterday we inserted two Recon Teams, call signs "Flat Foot" and "Happy Times" into this general area," he said, indicating an area southwest of Khe Sanh and about eighteen kilometers inside Laos from the north end of the Ashau Valley. "Flat Foot ran into trouble last evening. We thought they could break contact after darkness set in, but the NVA stayed after them."

"We tried a nighttime exfiltration with some Army choppers on temporary duty here, and a couple of Kingbees. The first slick got out with some of the team. The second one was shot down and a Kingbee was shot down. We had some Army gunships on station for fire support and attempted to get the rest of the team out with Jolly Greens. Again, the first one made it out with some of the team but got shot up pretty badly and crash-landed at Khe Sanh. The second Jolly Green was shot down with some of the team aboard. It's a mess and we're going to try and clean it up after first light."

With that, Major Snell turned the briefing over to the Operations Officer, Captain Billy R. Davis. Captain Davis was actually the team commander of Team A-323 from the First Special Forces Group in Okinawa. They were at Phu Bai on Temporary Duty (TDY) to augment our efforts. It was his team that would go into Laos on this rescue mission, but he wouldn't be accompanying them because he was the Camp Operations Officer. The Team was in the hands of the Executive Officer, 2LT. Rod Hoepner. Rod was junior to me so that left me, a senior Second Lieutenant, as the officer-in-charge on what was beginning to look like a classic goat rope. I considered Team A-323 to be my team now. What started as a bad feeling had now reached the "We who are about to die, salute you" stage. This was shaping up to be a "suicide" mission. Obviously the area was hot as a firecracker.

Captain Davis basically told all of us what we already knew by now. It wasn't much. There was heavy enemy activity and the area had been turned into a "flak-trap". (The NVA was fond of using downed aircraft and their crews, or surrounded SOG teams, as bait, knowing that rescue attempts would be made that would offer the NVA additional opportunities to shoot down more aircraft and kill more Americans). Three helicopters had been shot down and their crews were missing. That meant one VNAF crew of three, one Army crew of four and one Air Force crew of four. In addition, five of the original thirteen men on "Flat Foot" remained unaccounted for.

Aircraft in the area continued to hear Emergency Locator Beacons or "beepers", but did not have voice contact with anyone on the ground. In an effort not to lose more aircraft, our team would be landed several thousand meters from the crash sites. With that, we all broke into groups.

The pilots went off to do pilot stuff and "Top" Fisher, Lt. Hoepner, and I huddled around the counter to the S-2/3 (S-2 was the staff designation for Intelligence, S-3 for Operations) area to get more information, maps, and SOI's (Signal Operating Instructions). We were assigned call sign "Bull Dog" and told that our participation would last no longer than ten hours. We had to be out of the area by last light at all costs. Command in Saigon did not want to repeat another night of carnage. "Don't take food, clothing, excessive water or defensive weapons because you won't be there that long," we were told.

Our mission was to land the Cambodian Hatchet Force several thousand meters from the site of the previous action at first light, and work our way to the crash site(s), determine the fate of the helicopters and personnel and deal with the situation accordingly, remove any sensitive material, and get out. As usual, we were additionally tasked with killing enemy troops, taking prisoners, and seizing enemy equipment. Chances of heavy contact with NVA forces were deemed to be very probable.

It was pretty straightforward stuff. No details, no prior reconnaissance, and very little planning time. It was to be strictly an offensive mission. There was no mention of the weather and we didn't think to ask.

I stayed in the TOC to get more information and talk to the aircrews. Fisher and Hoepner went off to brief their team and oversee preparations for the "Red Devil" Battalion. The Red Devils were good soldiers but had never been on a cross border mission.

The Hatchet Force was ready and standing by on the helipad across from the camp entrance at 0600 (6 AM). The total Hatchet Force strength for this mission was close to ninety, a huge operation by SOG standards...and an indication of just how dangerous the area we are going into was considered to be.

It's obvious that the "powers that be", in this case probably CINCPAC (Commander in Chief of Pacific Forces), or maybe even the Whitehouse, weren't happy with the overall situation. Incidents of this nature were operational disasters and political nightmares. No doubt they are even less happy about sending in a large untried force under the command of a largely untried Second Lieutenant.

The Red Devil Hatchet Force is augmented by MSG. Charles "Skip" Minnicks, SFC. Robert Cavanaugh and SFC. Charlie Harper. "Skip" was a legendary SOG operative, and Cavanaugh and Harper were both very experienced. Minnicks and Cavanaugh were passing through camp on their way back from a mission debrief in Saigon. They were assigned to FOB 3 in Khe Sanh. When they heard that the Hatchet Force was going out to try and find Baxter and Kusick, they just attached themselves. Charlie Harper, assigned to

FOB 1, did the same. They didn't seek anyone's permission; they just got their rigs and went to the LZ west of the camp and waited for the choppers.

I don't doubt that they, and MSG Fisher, had been briefed to step in if they felt I was about to make a mistake. I was grateful for it. There wasn't room for egos when lives could be at stake. They were welcome additions to our merry little band and we could use all the help we could get.

It was the SOG way. Guys fought for seats on the choppers when there was trouble. In January of the next year I had to refuse Charlie Harper a seat on a Bright Light Mission to rescue Jim Coran. Jim was Charlie's brother-in-law. Charlie was almost in tears. Hell, I was almost in tears. Charlie understood and when I returned from the mission, Charlie and a couple of other well thought of NCO's got me drunk. That night was my war medal ceremony. Although I didn't actually ever get a medal, I got the approval of my NCO's and others for my combat performance. It meant more to me than anybody ever knew.

VI

The initial adrenaline surge was wearing off. We should have lifted off an hour and a half ago but we were in the "hurry up and wait" phase for which armies around the world are so famous. Confusion reigned and for the next couple of hours we were battered by conflicting orders and little information. There was no shade and we were sitting in the oily dirt of the helipad in chock order (Chock order is the order that the troops will be loaded in the aircraft) propped up by our rucksacks. It was getting hot!

The plan had been to board fourteen H-34 Helicopters (8 VNAF Kingbees and 6 from HMM-263, with 2 more Marine helicopters used as "Chase Ships" in the event that an aircraft is shot down or some other emergency arose during the insertion of Hatchet Force "Bull Dog") around 0600 Hours and fly into the LZ (Landing Zone) to the east-northeast of the crash sites, but the Marine helicopters had a previous mission to lift a Battalion from Camp Evens, west of Hue, to an area along Highway 1, the "Street without Joy", for a security sweep. It was now 0930 and they were just completing that mission.

The Kingbees and the Army helicopters on temporary duty at FOB 1 (UH-1C gunships using the call sign "Gladiator" and the remaining UH-1D "slick", call sign Spartan 52) had headed out to the area of operations (AO) at first light.

After the briefing earlier this morning, I was under the impression that a Kingbee had been shot down the night before and crashed. That was not what had happened. The Kingbee had indeed been "shot down", but had not crashed. It had sustained so much battle damage that it couldn't keep flying. The pilot managed to make a controlled landing in the jungles of Laos away from the immediate area of conflict. No one was injured in the landing and the VNAF crew of three, and three Nungs from "Flat Foot" whom they had rescued, spent a terrifying and uncomfortable night in the wilds of Laos. Because of communication difficulties, I would not know that until much later.

It turned out to be a good thing that our helicopters went back to the AO in Laos to look for their missing crews instead of picking up the Hatchet Force. They found the downed Kingbee, made a determination of what needed to be done, sent a couple of helicopters back to Da Nang for parts, returned to Laos, repaired the Kingbee and flew it out later in the day. Another helicopter flew their crew and our three Nungs back to Phu Bai.

Other Kingbees flew back to the crash sites and with the help of the "Gladiators" and A-1's on the scene, located the Aircraft Commander and Pilot from the downed Army UH-1D and rescued them. Army Warrant Officers Zanow and Woolridge were delivered to Phu Bai in separate VNAF Helicopters. Both were seriously injured and were taken into surgery immediately and couldn't be interviewed.

Survivors were scattered all over the AO (Area of Operations) in Laos and in Phu Bai and it became confusing to know how many people we needed to account for in Laos. It took hours to get everything sorted out. Word of the fate of the downed Kingbee didn't filter down to us until the operation was over. For years I didn't know the fate of the UH-1D Huey and thought the crew shot down the night of November 8/9, 1967, other than a survivor we would pick up later in the day, had perished. I didn't learn that Bill Woolridge and Kent Zanow had survived and been rescued until years later.

We eventually got a temporary "Stand Down" order and went back into the camp to find some shade and refill canteens. I went back to my room to get a can of C-Ration Peaches and stuck it in the pocket of my jungle fatigues. That turned out to be a smart move. I wish I had taken more. Then I went to the TOC to get any updates that might be available. Not unexpectedly, the situation is SNAFU'd (Situation Normal, All Fucked Up).

We were back on the helipad about 1100 hours and were told that the gaggle had been rounded up and as soon as all the helicopters (USMC and VNAF) were topped off with fuel they would pick us up and transport us to the landing zone in Laos.

Sure enough, a short while later we heard them lift off from Phu Bai Airfield just down the road. It was a short hop for them and they came roaring in causing the usual commotion and stirring up the oily dirt, which stuck to our sweaty bodies, further adding to our general discomfort. Hatchet Force "Bull Dog" loaded onto fourteen of the sixteen aircraft.

Two pairs of Echo Model Gunships growled in circles above the helipad. They were a welcome sight. The E Models were the Marine Corps' answer to the Army's C Model Huey Gunships. They were a little heavier than the Army Gunships because of extra instrumentation and navigational aids. That would help us in the days to come. They didn't carry quite as much ordnance as the Army, but they were very effective and well flown by courageous pilots.

The Kingbees came in first and I was the last man on the first helicopter so I could be the first off when we reach our LZ. The Marine H-34's followed the Kingbees, picking up the remaining Hatchet Force members.

And suddenly, we were away. After hours of waiting in the hot sun, we climbed into the cool air at 5000 feet. There were some serious mountains to cross on our way to the AO.

It wasn't long before we were over the A Shau Valley, that forbidding place known to us as the "Valley of Death". It was almost always covered in ground fog and the giant defoliated trees would poke up through the mist like skeleton fingers trying to snatch helicopters from the sky. It was almost always wet in A Shau Valley and the ceiling was usually low, making air operations difficult and dangerous. The NVA had been moving some heavy anti-aircraft guns into the valley and it was disconcerting to be flying over and be buffeted by flak. It was definitely a place of nightmares.

A short time later, the VNAF Crew Chief tugged on my sleeve and pointed to the LZ. Having never seen it before, it took me a minute to locate it and reconcile it with my map.

Then I noticed the burned areas to the west and saw the smoke. Men had lost their lives here and no doubt a clever and determined enemy waited for us. The bad feeling surfaced again, but was quickly overtaken by the world's greatest "high". If real life were like the movies, this is where "Ride of the Valkyries" by Richard Wagner, or better yet, the last guitar/horn riff in "Liberation" by Chicago, would fade in as background music.

There is no way to adequately describe the adrenaline dump that accompanies a combat air assault. It happens every time, no matter how many times you do it. And every time I've thought to myself, "If I could just find a way to recreate this as a thrill ride at Disneyland it would be the ultimate E-Ticket Ride. I would be a billionaire." But it couldn't be done. There was nothing to compare to this.

Sometimes the helicopter came screaming in at treetop level, suddenly flaring, and plopping down in a small jungle clearing, barely stopping before it powered away over the treetops. You had a few seconds to get away from the machine before it killed you and then you faced whatever fate had in store for you on that particular day. Other times it was different...but the same.

This time, we approached the LZ at a very high altitude because of concern for enemy antiaircraft and ground fire. We were directly over the LZ when suddenly the bottom fell out and we were in a death spiral toward a large grassy area on a ridgeline east of the smoking areas. Although we were hanging on to anything we could for dear life, there was no need; centrifugal force had us pinned inside the aircraft. There was no sound. The engine was at idle and it seemed our fate was now ruled by basic physics. We were going to die! All I could hear was silence.

Spang! A bullet passed through the tail boom. It didn't matter because we were dead men. Suddenly the engine roared to life and our life ending crash became a little bump. Whomp! We were on the ground and I was out. My exit was not elegant, but it got the job done. The eighty pounds of extra weight I was carrying didn't help. The Kingbee was gone, but the roaring continued as the remaining thirteen helicopters disgorged their loads and passed over me, looking like enraged dragonflies and sounding like storm driven waves crashing on the North Shore of Oahu.

The Recon teams had some clever tactics to disguise their insertions using a high helicopter which could be seen descending toward an LZ, while another helicopter, flying nap of the earth, inserted the team at a different LZ. The high bird sometimes left a "Nightingale Device" on the fake LZ. The Nightingale Device simulated a fire fight and drew enemy troops to the fake LZ. If fighters were available they might bomb the fake LZ after the device went off. The recon teams could play a "Shell Game" with the enemy by "inserting" into multiple LZ's so the enemy had to guess which one was the real insertion. The objective of reconnaissance is to remain undetected and gather intelligence. The recon teams were small and tried to avoid combat.

But there was no way to "sneak" a Hatchet or Havoc force into an area. The mission of the Hatchet Force was different from the reconnaissance patrols. HF's by and large sought combat by joining a fight in progress or seeking out the enemy for the purposes of combat. Secrecy was rarely possible because of the size of the force.

I indicated to the men around me to face the tree line to the east. If there was immediate trouble, it would come from there. It had grown quiet. No helicopter noise, no voices, and no gunfire. The LZ was cold. I enjoyed the silence, a rare thing in combat operations. We got accustomed to the jungle noises for a moment.

"Covey, this is Bulldog, over."

"Bulldog, Covey. Go."

"Covey, Bulldog, the LZ is cold. We are moving to the crash site now, over."

SFC Dudley Nutter, the FOB 1 "Covey Rider" sitting in the right seat of the O-2, next to the pilot, Captain Corwin "Kip" Kippenhan, responded, "Roger Bulldog. We still have "beepers", but no voice contact, over."

They had flown all day the day before when "Flat Foot" and "Happy Times" had been inserted and had barely gotten back to Da Nang when they re-launched to return to the area to guide the rescue efforts. In addition to the long hours, "Kip", was suffering from severe stomach cramps.

Last night, they had been relieved by another Covey, probably Covey 57, working out of Khe Sanh about 0100 local time, just after Jolly Green 29 cleared the area. They returned to Phu Bai for a brief rest. They were back in the area just after first light this morning. Captain Kippenhan, SFC. Nutter, and the other FAC's and Covey riders who participated in this action were definitely some of the many unsung heroes in this incident.

VII

General Eisenhower said, "Plans are everything before the battle begins, but once the shooting started plans were worthless." Hatchet Force "Bull Dog" didn't have a plan, but they had a mission, and it was to get to the crash sites, do what they could, and get out of town by sundown. They would have to go with General Patton's response to "Ike". "Victory…will depend on Execution, not Plans." It was just as well, we never had a chance to make plans on the Hatchet Force. We just reacted.

The leaders of "Bull Dog" were finally seeing the terrain from the ground and it was problematical. We didn't have a lot of time; thanks to the extremely late start we got, and would have to cross a lot of open ground to get to the crash sites because time was of the essence.

A quick meeting of the "Bull Dog Brain Trust" confirmed everyone's concerns. Because the ground was so open along the necessary route of movement, there would have to be security along the ridge top that paralleled the main force movement and the high ground over-looking the crash sites would have to be cleared of possible enemy. MSG. "Skip" Minnicks started out with his two Americans and a small element of Cambodian mercenaries to secure the ridge.

The main force was moving east from the landing zone through knee-high Elephant Grass. It is ubiquitous to the warmer climates of Africa and Asia, and is a tough, fibrous grass that can grow twenty feet tall in stands thick enough to slow, and sometimes deflect, bullets. In this case, however, it offered no cover or concealment.

Everyone within ten kilometers knew "Bull Dog" was here and everyone within five kilometers knew exactly where "Bull Dog" was…they were watching. I couldn't have felt more exposed if I were standing naked on the fifty-yard line of the Super Bowl during halftime. I didn't expect to make it to the crash site(s) before we were hit by mortars or heavy automatic fire. Our only advantage was to stay on high ground as long as possible. We were thankful for the obvious presence of Covey, the helicopters, and the A-1's. They were real deterrents to enemy attack.

As Lloyd Fisher recalls:

"After getting off the LZ we sent Minnick's security element and part of our Cambodian Battalion to the top of the ridge line that ran parallel down from the hilltop. We then proceeded to move thru the elephant grass towards the ravine (crash site) and hilltop. My recall is vague on when the gunship was located but I think it was while we were moving to the crash site. I seem to remember someone reporting finding the Huey and we said, 'Good, destroy it.' Our primary concern was getting to the JG and we were short on time.

As we got close to the ravine (tree-line) I found a trail in the elephant grass showing bloodstains and 1st aid bandages on the ground. Knowing it was a US type I followed it down-hill until it was reported that the crewman or pilot had walked out. I had some bodes with me during this time. This was all taking time from getting to the JG site.

We then decided that the hilltop overlooking the crash site had to be cleared before sending anyone across the open area to the crash site. I/we took a small element of bodes over the ridgeline and down behind the hill. We then proceeded to scale the back of that damn hill, which was nearly vertical, but we made it and were satisfied that we now had the high ground overlooking the site.

By the way, when Ron Bock and I returned to that site in 2003 with the Joint Task Force for Full Accounting (Hawaii), that damn hill was the first thing I spotted from the Chopper. The vertical back made it stand out from all surrounding terrain features."

(A field team from the Task Force for Full Accounting first visited the area of the USAF HH-3E Jolly Green tail number 66-13279 and U.S. Army UH-1D tail number 66-00847 crash sites in January of 1995 to search for remains of American military men lost on the night of November 8th and 9th, 1967. They were unable to locate the sites, but did learn of a possible witness who was due to return to the area in March. The team returned in March, and with the help of the witness, located both crash sites. While they found equipment consistent with both types of aircraft, they found no human remains or personal equipment.

Lloyd Fisher and Ronald Bock returned to the crash site with another field team in 2003. Again no human remains or personal equipment was found. Lloyd and Ron reported that the team made an extensive excavation and they felt no stone had been left unturned.)

Within minutes of leaving the LZ, a blond headed man wearing olive drab stateside fatigues was spotted coming up a grassy draw toward the main body of the Hatchet Force. He was Specialist 4 Richard Jarvis, the gunner on the U.S. Army UH-1D "Huey" shot down the previous evening. The Army helicopters, 2 UH-1D transports using the call sign "Spartan" and 2 UH-1C gunships using the call sign "Gladiator" were from the 190th Assault Helicopter Company (AHC).

Although stationed at Bien Hoa, near Saigon, the 190th had been temporarily assigned to support the Marines in I Corp. This is the same Helicopter Company that had transported me in and out of the mission last week. The Company had returned to Bien Hoa several days before, leaving two "slicks" and two gunships behind to support FOB 1.

Jarvis seemed to be in pretty good shape, considering what he had been through. I asked him about the rest of the crew and the location of the downed Huey. He said everyone else was injured, and he thought Bill Whitney, the Crew Chief, was dead. He had been with Warrant Officer Bill Zanow for a while during the night hiding at the bottom of the hill, but Zanow was badly injured and not able to get up the hill to high ground, so he sent Jarvis up the hill to get help. Jarvis thinks both Zanow and Warrant Officer Kent Woolridge, the Aircraft Commander of Spartan 53, were picked up earlier in the day but he didn't know if they were alive. (VNAF Kingbees picked up Zanow and

Woolridge separately and transported them to Phu Bai.)

Specialist Jarvis also told me about a heavy machine gun on the other side of the valley. He was a sharp kid and gave me good information that paid off later. A helicopter was called to evacuate Jarvis and "Bull Dog" moved on.

The main force of "Bull Dog" proceeded to an area of burned "Elephant Grass" near the southwestern side of Hill 891 (so named because it is 891 meters in elevation). There were two partially burned bodies there. They were carrying some U.S. equipment and both Fisher and I especially noted the K-Bar knife, which was issued to all U.S. Marines. There was also a pair of U.S. binoculars.

We both initially thought the bodies were Americans because of the American equipment. MSG. Fisher read my mind when he said, "Poor Bastards." They turned out to be dead NVA soldiers, and they had almost certainly seen combat against our Marines. War is an ugly thing and people die. Better the NVA than us!

I removed a boot from one of the dead NVA. It was canvas with a rubber sole. I had been briefed by the S-2 (Intelligence) to bring back examples of enemy footgear when possible. Just as James Bond had "Q", SOG had a CIA run group in Taiwan that provided all sorts of unique weapons and items with which we could fight, and subvert, the VC and NVA. One of their on-going projects was to equip our recon teams with footgear that would leave the same boot print as an NVA boot, hence the need to have current examples of enemy boot treads. (At one point, they even produced a boot sole that left an impression of a bare foot.)

Fisher removed the U.S. binoculars. They were pretty smoked up…like looking through tinted glass, but they magnified and they might be useful.

He then left with a small force to sweep around the backside (north side) of Hill 891 to make sure it was clear of enemy soldiers. On the map it didn't look too bad and should not take him long if he didn't run into trouble. The map lied…it was a cliff, muddy and very steep. He and his group had their hands full and it was a tough climb to the top of the hill from the north side.

I started to the front (south side) of the hilltop with the main body of troops. We could reinforce Fisher if need be.

"Skip" Minnicks and his group found the Army "Huey" crash site. They destroyed weapons, ammunition, radios, and anything else that might be useful to the enemy. Nearby, they found the body of Sgt. Bill Whitney, the much beloved Crew Chief of Spartan 53. He died of wounds sometime during the interim between his helicopter being shot down and the arrival of the Hatchet Force. His M-60 Machine Gun was in his lap. He was the first member of the 190th AHC to be killed in Vietnam.

Minnicks called for a helicopter to evacuate Whitney's body and the sad and badly flawed process of returning him home began. His remains would be lost for over 30 days in the confusion of being an Army crewman, far from his parent unit, and sent to a Marine

Corp facility. The demands of the moment required his friends and fellow crewmen to press on and he was sent on without any acknowledgement of his bravery, although he was posthumously awarded a Distinguished Flying Cross

Once that sad task was complete, Minnicks and his group started across the face of the hill to catch up with the rest of us. The transport helicopters returned to Phu Bai, but the Marine gunships remained over us by cycling through Khe Sanh for fuel and armament. They were a comfort. In our haste to accomplish the mission, we got spread out and we were expecting an attack.

Fisher and his group were climbing the north side of Hill 891. We were all in a hurry to find the Jolly Green crash site. We didn't have much time until it became dark and we were all cognizant of the requirement to be out of there by nightfall. I started down the hill toward the tree line with the main force. Lloyd's group had swept the hilltop and was not far behind and "Skip" had almost caught up. I would be glad to have everyone "rejoined".

Lloyd found a blood trail and some U.S. bandages. His group was following the trail when he spotted a pen flare and the gunships reported seeing another American in a flight suit emerging from the tree line some distance from us. We all turned in that direction. The gunship radioed that he was almost out of fuel and thought he might be light enough to land and pick the survivor up.

(Many helicopters were underpowered. Depending on weight, altitude, heat, and humidity, they were sometimes unable to land or hover in the mountains of Laos until they had reduced their weight by burning fuel or pitching equipment overboard. Pilots carefully computed what was known as the "Density Altitude Factor" when planning their flights.)

The gunship crew, after jettisoning as much weight as they could, including rocket pods and extra machine gun ammo, made the pick-up and we learned that the new survivor was the pilot of Jolly Green-26, Captain Gerald Young. The gunships left the area and those of us on the ground resumed our search for the Jolly Green crash site with renewed vigor. If Captain Young survived, maybe there are other survivors! Captain Young would later be awarded the Congressional Medal of Honor for his actions on the night of November 8/9, 1967. This entire incident would be one of the most highly decorated incidents of the Vietnam War for the United States Air Force.

Lt. Col. Gerald O. Young

**The President of the United States
in the name of The Congress
takes pleasure in presenting the
Medal of Honor
to**

YOUNG, GERALD O.

Rank and organization: Captain, U.S. Air Force, 37th ARS Da Nang AFB, Republic of Vietnam. *Place and Date:* Khesanh, 9 November 1967. *Entered service at:* Colorado Springs, Colo. *Born:* 9 May 1930, Chicago, Ill.

Citation:
For conspicuous gallantry and intrepidity at the risk of his life above and beyond the call of duty. Capt. Young distinguished himself while serving as a helicopter rescue crew commander. Capt. Young was flying escort for another helicopter attempting the night rescue of an Army ground reconnaissance team in imminent danger of death or capture. Previous attempts had resulted in the loss of 2 helicopters to hostile ground fire. The endangered team was positioned on the side of a steep slope which required unusual airmanship on the part of Capt. Young to effect pickup. Heavy automatic weapons fire from the surrounding enemy severely damaged 1 rescue

helicopter, but it was able to extract 3 of the team. The commander of this aircraft recommended to Capt. Young that further rescue attempts be abandoned because it was not possible to suppress the concentrated fire from enemy automatic weapons. With full knowledge of the danger involved, and the fact that supporting helicopter gunships were low on fuel and ordnance, Capt. Young hovered under intense fire until the remaining survivors were aboard. As he maneuvered the aircraft for takeoff, the enemy appeared at point-blank range and raked the aircraft with automatic weapons fire. The aircraft crashed, inverted, and burst into flames. Capt. Young escaped through a window of the burning aircraft. Disregarding serious burns, Capt. Young aided one of the wounded men and attempted to lead the hostile forces away from his position. Later, despite intense pain from his burns, he declined to accept rescue because he had observed hostile forces setting up automatic weapons positions to entrap any rescue aircraft. For more than 17 hours he evaded the enemy until rescue aircraft could be brought into the area. Through his extraordinary heroism, aggressiveness, and concern for his fellow man, Capt. Young reflected the highest credit upon himself, the U.S. Air Force, and the Armed Forces of his country.

The terrain was deceptive and as we entered the dense vegetation in the tree line we were channeled into a deep gully. It was about a yard wide at the bottom and maybe 3 yards wide at the top. There was no evidence that a helicopter had crashed there. It was the wrong ravine. And it was dangerous. One enemy soldier with grenades and an automatic weapon at the top of the gully could damn near wipe us out. I radioed the others not to follow us.

The 15 to 20 foot sides of the gully were steep and un-climbable for a large force of untrained mercenaries such as ours. It would take too long to get out that way. Heavy brush grew over us, the sun was going down and it was getting dark at the bottom of the gully. The air in the gully was fetid and I felt stifled. It was possible that no human beings had ever walked this gully. I could understand why. We needed to get out of there.

A Soc Chan (we called him Sam), the Cambodian Battalion Commander and our lead interpreter made his way to me, looking scared and concerned. "Sir," he said, "this is not a good place. The soldiers are very scared. We must leave this place."

I agreed and told him we were looking for a way out. I looked back at the line of Cambodian mercenaries behind me. They were Buddhists. They were very superstitious and they were quite intuitive. Every one of them wore an amulet on a leather thong around his neck. The amulets were little bags, usually made from a small square of red bandana, containing grains of rice and other tiny objects that had been blessed by a Buddhist Priest. When they were scared or stressed, they would touch the bags in much the same way that devout Catholics fingered their Rosary Beads.

Every one of the soldiers that I could see had his "Prayer Bag" in his mouth! For the first time that day I felt true fear rather than the usual dose of healthy apprehension. I quickly suppressed it and moved on.

We continued down the gully for another 50 meters or so and finally found a way out on the east side of the gully. Unfortunately, we wanted to go west, so we had to go back up the hill to the beginning of the gully where we could cross to the west and help look for the crash site of Jolly Green-26. The hill was steep and slippery. With the added weight of our rucksacks, it was a tough climb.

Covey reported a "Beeper" in a heavily wooded area about 600 meters southeast of where Captain Young was picked up. Someone in the Air Force Chain of Command wanted us to check it out. I thought that would be a particularly bad idea. We could not get to the location before it turned dark and it was in the opposite direction of the Jolly Green crash site. I decided our best move was to keep looking for the site of the downed Jolly Green. Odds were good that the "Beeper" was a trap. A voice on the radio said, "Cowards!" I'd like to meet that guy some day! I informed Covey that we would continue to the Jolly Green crash site.

The light was fading fast and we had not found the JG crash site. Keeping in mind that I was told to be out of the area at last light at all costs, I radioed Covey, who was still in the area. Two Marine gunships were back as well.

"Covey, Bulldog, over."

"Bull Dog, Covey, go ahead."

"Covey, it'll be dark soon. I don't think we will reach the JG site before dark. We're going to find a PZ (Pick up zone), over."

"Bull Dog, Covey, stand by, over."

After several minutes, Covey called back with the news that we couldn't be picked up because a severe storm (it was actually a typhoon) had moved into the coastal areas of South Viet Nam, including Phu Bai, and all the helicopters were grounded due to weather and visibility. We were advised to find a good location to RON (Remain overnight). They would come for us at first light tomorrow.

There was nothing to do but to climb to the top of Hill 891 and prepare a night defensive position as best we could. We had few defensive armaments; no food, not much water, and many of the soldiers had nothing to protect them from the elements other than the clothes on their backs. It would be a cold night in the mountains of Laos at best. At worst, it wouldn't matter. We began our trek up the hillside in the fading light.

THUMP! A small explosion in the column behind me, and a really bad situation just got worse. SFC. Osborne has just stepped on a "Toe Popper" and it has taken half his foot off and injured his lower leg.

A number of us passed over the mine, but "Ozzie" was the unlucky one who stepped on it. I called Covey and asked for a Med-Evac, not really expecting to get one, but about a half hour later a Huey (Spartan 52) hovered into our hastily prepared LZ near the top of Hill 891. The sun had set and it was almost completely dark.

SGT. Ron Bock, the Medic had done such a great job with SFC. Osborne, that the Doctors at Phu Bai were able to save enough of his foot so that he would walk again. Ron had also been caring for a very young Cambodian who was suffering from stomach cramps. He was also evacuated on the Huey and at the last minute another Cambodian soldier jumped on just as the helicopter lifted off.

At first, Ron thought the guy was "bugging out", but on reflection he realized that Sam, the Cambodian Commander, had ordered him to go to look after the sick Cambodian. Indigenous casualties were transferred to Vietnamese Hospitals for treatment. That was a real problem for our Nungs and Cambodians. They were minorities and racism was alive and well in Vietnam. If the young Cambodian went into a Vietnamese facility alone, there was a good chance he might not come out, so Sam sent along a bodyguard.

In the rapidly fading light, the gunships which had returned from Khe Sanh after delivering Jerry Young to the medics, contacted me, saying that they were almost "Bingo" on fuel and would be leaving in a few minutes. I direct them to expend their ordinance on the heavy automatic weapon location described to me by Specialist Jarvis. They put rockets and machine gun fire into the dark shadows of the cliff to our south. There was no return fire. Odd!

It was inky dark. As the gunships flew over us, they requested that we mark our perimeter for future reference. We displayed strobe lights at the east and west limits of the perimeter. A door gunner on one of the gunships opened up on the strobe thinking it was ground fire. One of the "Bodes" was wounded. Great! We wouldn't be able to get him out tonight, so Ron went to work stabilizing him and making him as comfortable as possible for the long night ahead. The gunship pilot apologized profusely and bid us good luck. The gunships flew off in the direction of Khe Sanh.

It was now completely dark and Lloyd Fisher and I stood atop hill 891 looking into a clear velvety black sky. The stars were appearing. At first there were hundreds, then thousands, then millions. The normally taciturn Master Sergeant Fisher stole my thoughts again when he said, "Sir this is really bad."

I replied, "Top, I'll be surprised if we see another sunrise."

I sensed him nodding his head as he said, "Yep."

His reply was eloquent in its simplicity. We would fight with all our beings until we were killed. Then it would be someone else's turn to come for us. We silently made peace with whomever, or whatever, we believed and prepared for what lay ahead.

VIII

Hatchet Force "Bull Dog" had not brought entrenching tools, food, or extra water, but they were preparing for a night defense of Hill 891. It was difficult to dig in the clay soil with our hands but that's about all we had. We only had two machine guns, one claymore mine (thanks to Rick Bayer, the Demolitions Sergeant), and we had no mortars. This was not the Boy Scouts and we were not prepared. I should have known better.

We occupied the military crest of the hill (the area just below the top of the hill). To our south the hill was relatively steep and open. This was the area of the hill where the helicopters tried to pick up "Flat Foot". I marveled that they didn't have rotor strikes against the hillside during their night landings. It would be really tricky in the daytime, but a night landing here, under heavy fire, was an incredible feat of exceptional airmanship.

A hundred meters down-slope the tree line began and covered the rest of the steep downslope. Off to the southwest, was the tree line that concealed the Jolly Green-26 crash site. Although these tree lines were now dark and foreboding, they were not the greatest threat.

To our east and west, the slopes were gentler and trees extended almost to our perimeter. They were the most likely avenues of enemy approach. We placed the machine guns there and concentrated more of the force on the east and west ends of the perimeter.

To the north was the slippery cliff-like slope that MSG. Fisher and his group climbed earlier today. It was there that we set up the CP (Command Post). I had respect for the NVA and knew that they often used the most difficult, hence the least guarded, approach to their objective. We were vastly out-numbered here and time was on the enemy's side. I wanted to be sure this approach was constantly guarded, so Lloyd and I would do it ourselves. The position also offered protection from direct fire from the other approaches, thus protecting the all-important radio.

Nights in the mountains of Laos got cold. Lloyd's poncho and liner were wrapped around "Ozzie" when he was med-evaced earlier. So we shared mine. We were lucky to have something to keep the dew off us and to give us a little warmth. Since we believed we would be exfiltrated in the morning, I opened the can of C-Ration Peaches and shared them with Lloyd.

"Bull Dog, Bull Dog, this is Blind Bat Zero Three, over." After several hours of silence on the radio, this unexpected call startled me.

"Bull Dog, Bull Dog, this is Blind Bat Zero Three, over."

I responded, "Blind Bat Zero Three, this is Bull Dog, over."

"Bull Dog, Bat Three is inbound to your location to turn on the lights, over."

"Ahh...roger that. Say again your intention, over."

"Bull Dog, Bat Three is a flare ship. Just say the word and we will turn your night into day. It'll be so bright down there you will be able to read the fine print on your Divorce Papers, over."

We could now hear the drone of the approaching C-130. Within a few minutes, we were adjusting Blind Bat 03's flare patterns and as advertised, it was as bright as day around our perimeter.

The flares came every few minutes in strings of three. We could hear the pop when the detonators ignited the flares and they sizzled and smoked like Fourth of July sparklers as they floated down under their small parachutes. They were Magnesium Flares and burned with a white-hot intensity that took away the night. They swung back and forth as they came down, giving the illusion that the trees and the grass were living, animated beings. The shadows jumped back and forth and the landscape became surreal in the constantly moving bright lights. The woods were full of ghosts.

But the light was comforting and served to keep the enemy from massing too close to our perimeter. Blind Bat-03 had indeed taken away the night.

Even more comforting was the voice on the radio. We were fully expecting an enemy attack and we believed that we were in danger of being overrun. The voice high in the darkness kept us talking. It was nice to know that if the end came, there would be a witness to our last battle.

Lloyd and I took turns on the radio. I can only speak for myself, but I suspect many of us on that mountainside in Laos had the same thought process regarding the hours to come. I moved rapidly through the five stages of grief and was ready to fight and die if necessary.

Denial...this can't be happening. We were supposed to have been out of here hours ago.

Anger...this thing is so screwed up. If I survive this I am going back to camp and kick some serious ass, because I'm definitely too young to die!

Bargaining...this was bizarre, I remember specifically saying to myself that if I survived, I would go home and wash the dishes every night... I lied.

Regret...I think of all the opportunities I've blown and all the girls in my life who I foolishly let slip away. Each of them was wonderful and unique and deserved better treatment than they got from me. I had fond thoughts and profound regrets about all of them. But mostly, I regretted that I probably would never see my family and the little blind date girl again. It was the loneliest feeling I've ever had

Acceptance...I would probably die on this unnamed spot on the side of a hill in Laos; but by God, the people who killed me were going to know I was there, and they would pay a heavy price for taking me out. By this time I was at peace and I had no fear!

It was not false bravado; it's just the way it was. The whole process took only a few minutes. Once death was accepted as not just possible, but inevitable; fear of death was banished and a sense of peace set in that made me very lethal and dangerous. It was intense and scared me a little bit.

I became much too busy to dwell on my personal thoughts and problems. There was work to be done. It would be wet (bloody) and dark and dirty. We were SOG...this is what we did.

Blind Bat-03 continued to talk to us and to take away our darkness. At one point, the voice in the sky asked if we were a big force or a small force. For a moment, I was at a loss for the answer. For a SOG operation, we were extremely large, but surrounded by thousands of NVA, we felt much too small. If the NVA were listening, and they most assuredly were, I don't want them to think that overrunning us will be easy.

I answered, "We're a large force."

The Bat responded, "That's good because it looks like a Boy Scout Jamboree down there. You guys are surrounded by hundreds of camp fires."

I answered the Bat, "If this turns out badly, will you get word to my unit that I want my parents and my girl to know that my last thoughts were of them?"

The Bat promised that he would do it if necessary.

To our east-southeast we saw a steady stream of lights. Judging from the movement and brightness of the lights, we thought they were trucks. A footpath showed on our map at about 4000 meters in that direction. The Bat couldn't see them, but called for some A-1's using the call sign "Pedro". "Pedro" didn't see them either and couldn't safely come down into the valley to see them from our perspective because of the terrain, so the NVA got a pass and would live to die elsewhere someday. I don't know why I didn't think of "Skyspot".

The NVA were very proficient with their road building and camouflage. They used trellises to train and secure the second and third canopies of foliage over their roads and trails making the paths invisible from the air. It was obvious to us that they had expanded the footpath into a roadway and cleverly camouflaged it from aerial observation. The lights continued to move even with the aircraft overhead and the flares to their west. After counting several hundred lights we lost interest. The lights continued all night long.

After several hours, Lloyd and I agreed that maybe we should turn out the lights. Although we were surprised that we had not been attacked yet, we wanted to be sure that if an attack came, there would be enough flares to light the battlefield.

Lloyd passed that decision to the Bat and the Bat responded, "We were going to suggest that. We're going to go west a little bit to check something out, but if you need us we'll only be a few minutes away."

The drone of the C-130 faded off to the west and we were alone in the dark. Our night vision began to return. All remained quiet.

A short while later the Bat was back and informed us that there were heavy anti-aircraft guns to the southwest being moved in our direction. The area was a little hot for them so they would orbit in our area until their replacement flare ship arrived.

"Bull Dog, Bat Zero Three, over."

"This is Bull Dog, go ahead."

"Bat Three, we're about ready to RTB (Return to Base). Lamplighter will take over for us. We have briefed him and he should be on station in a few minutes. Good luck, Bull Dog...you may need it. And don't worry, I'll check back and if I need to relay your message, I will. Blind Bat, out."

"Lamplighter" was the call sign of another group of Air Force C-130 flare ships. "Blind Bat" and "Lamplighter" were from the same unit at Ubon Royal Thai Air Base (RTAB). All the flare ships were assigned to the 374th Tactical Airlift Wing at Naha Air Base, Okinawa. They were TDY for 180 days under the control of the 8th Tactical Fighter Wing at Ubon RTAB, Thailand. Each crew would fly 14 to 16 missions a month (they were limited to 120 flying hours a month). 5 missions a night were flown, three Blind Bat and two Lamplighters. Usually Blind Bat was over southern Laos and Lamplighter was over northern Laos and North Vietnam. Most nights they flew hunter-killer missions on the trail looking for anything that moved and anti-aircraft gun positions.

"Alley Cat" and "Moonbeam", were Airborne Battle Command and Control Center (ABCCC) C-130s, would, on occasion, direct them to other targets/areas where their assistance was needed for rescues or to support what they called "road teams"---Special Forces on the ground.

"Bull Dog, Bull Dog, this is Lamplighter, Lamplighter, over."

"Lamplighter, Bull Dog, go ahead"

"Bull Dog, we're in the area and we want to kick out a flare for you to adjust, over."

"Roger, Lamplighter. Go ahead."

We didn't hear a plane and we didn't see a flare. We reported this to Lamplighter.

"Roger, Bull Dog. We'll drop another flare."

Nothing.

This went on for about fifteen minutes and Lamplighter was getting more and more agitated. We lit up a strobe light, but Lamplighter saw nothing. Finally I asked Lamplighter, "Lamplighter, this is Bull Dog. Do you see a lot of campfires?"

The answer was negative.

Lamplighter widened his orbit and eventually we heard the drone of his engines and vectored him into our general area. He had been looking for us many miles away. Lloyd requested that he hold his flares. If we were hit with a ground attack, Lamplighter would know by the tracers. If he saw tracers, turn on the lights.

The calming rapport that we had with Blind Bat was gone. The radio remained silent except for a call from "Alley Cat", requesting a SitRep (Situation Report) and "Iron Spud", an Army Mohawk Surveillance Aircraft from the 131st Aviation Company in Phu Bai. "Alley

Cat", "Moon Beam", and "Iron Spud" would always check on teams in the field at night. It was comforting to know that someone would eventually establish contact during the dark, lonely nights in Laos. If nothing else, it would help establish a time of death.

We had devised a squelch code for times when the enemy was nearby, and it would be too dangerous to even whisper. The aircraft checking on us would ask specific questions and we would respond by pressing the talk switch on our radio a specified number of times depending on what the answer was.

I told both aircraft that our situation was static. Although we were surrounded, we had not been attacked.

And then, the one thing that we thought would not happen, did. It was imperceptible at first. The sky in the east began to lighten. It was a dangerous time on the battlefield. Defender's senses are dulled and alertness wanes. The enemy frequently attacked during the hours just before dawn. The American team members brought the perimeter to full alert, preparing for an assault that would never come. We made it through the night. Now all we had to do is finish the mission by finding and processing the Jolly Green 26 crash site and then get picked up and flown back to Phu Bai for the traditional breakfast of steak and eggs that the Mess Sergeant always prepared for returning teams.

A delicious thought that obviously was not going to pan out. As the sky in the east became lighter, we could see huge banks of clouds. Helicopters would be unable to reach us today. We were at the mercy of the enemy and the elements. It was time to worry about the things we could control, not the things we couldn't.

Breakfast wasn't an issue. We had no food. Most of us hadn't eaten since dinner two nights ago. Our water supply was low, but we didn't believe thirst would become a problem. In a few hours we would probably have more water than we needed. The clouds were blowing toward us. There was already a high overcast above us.

The "Brain Trust" made a plan. We would split the force. One group, with some of the Senior NCO's and Lt. Hoepner, would find the Jolly Green crash site. I would keep a force to secure the top of the hill, maintain communications, and act as reinforcement if the troops at the crash site ran into trouble.

It was time to go to work.

IX

The clouds were moving in quickly and the ceiling was lowering. Not only would we be stuck here, but we also wouldn't be getting any air support or resupply for a while due to the worsening weather. We were really vulnerable. A light drizzle started just after the group going in search of the Jolly Green 26 crash site disappeared into the tree line a hundred meters or so to our southwest.

Those of us manning the hilltop consolidated the perimeter and put out Observation Posts to our east and west. The mountaintop to our south was now shrouded in clouds. The drizzle softened the clay soil somewhat and we were able to dig a little deeper. Unfortunately water collected in the bottom of the holes and made the prospect of the coming night just a little more miserable...if we were still there. Our situation could only have been worse if we were under attack. I kept wondering why we weren't. What were they waiting for; they had all the advantages and we are so vulnerable? Our force was split, the weather was bad, there would be no air support, and they out-numbered us by thousands.

In my opinion there might have been several factors working in our favor:

Our force was larger than the usual rescue force and the NVA may not have been prepared to deal with us initially. They were set up around the crash site prepared to shoot down more rescue helicopters and supporting aircraft or to ambush a small rescue team. Our large insertion may have caught them unaware and unprepared.

Initially, the enemy troops in the area seemed to be on a mission and could not afford the time nor the resources to deal with us. They were listening to our radio transmissions and knew that our mission was to rescue and recover. They correctly guessed that we would try to avoid enemy contact. They were satisfied with containing us and continuing their mission. They would take what they could get without suffering too many losses. If we made a serious mistake, they would exploit it.

Blind Bat had told us the NVA were moving serious anti-aircraft guns in our direction. They may have wanted to keep us relatively intact to use as bait for another big score. It might have taken the NVA several days to bring in, and position, a force large enough to engage us and our supporting aircraft. If the weather stayed bad for several days, it would negate our air power advantage and give the NVA time to set up a "Flak Trap" which would improve their odds of overrunning us and taking out more aircraft.

"Flat Foot", "Happy Times", and later "Bull Dog" landed near the transportation corridor that the NVA designated B-45. B-45 was part of Route 922 and Route 92 which was an east-west connector route between the main north-south corridor of the Ho Chi Minh Trail and the upper reaches of the A Shau Valley. The Route 922 was not a single road, but a loose collection of trails and roads.

The Communist High Command in Hanoi divided the South into five military fronts (B1, B2, B3, B4, and B5). Headquarters B4 Front commanded NVA regular forces in Thua Thien Province and the portion of Quang Tri Province south of National Highway 9. The B-45 corridor was a very important strategic line of communication and transportation for the B-4 Front. In early November 1967, the NVA was in the midst of pushing men and material into the B4 Front and the Khe Sanh area (B5 Front) in preparation for the 1968 Tet offensive.

NVA forces along this corridor reacted quickly and forcefully to any threat to this important corridor...and the NVA regarded reconnaissance teams as very serious threats. These factors helped explain why "Flat Foot" and the rescue forces encountered such difficulty in the area. "Flat Foot" was the proverbial stick poking the hornet's nest with the usual result.

U.S. Intelligence would later learn that the North Vietnamese were moving major NVA units, including the 325C, 304 and 320 NVA Divisions plus a regiment of the 324 Division, through Laos into South Vietnam in November 1967.

The previous evening, Covey 51 flew low over the site to help us locate it this morning. His description of JG-26 at that time was, "70 to 80 pounds of molten metal."

By mid-morning the Rescue/Recovery element was at the JG-26 crash site. Almost immediately SFC Bruce Luttrell found the Flight Deck of JG-26. He could make out two bodies, imbedded in the wreckage. Identification couldn't be positively made in the field, but Dog Tags on the remains indicated that the two were Captain Ralph Brower, the co-pilot of JG-26 and Staff Sergeant Eugene Clay, the Flight Engineer.

While the team Medic, Ron Bock, began the grisly and painstaking task of removing the remains of two U.S. military men from the wreckage of the big Sikorsky CH-3 Jolly Green Giant helicopter, other members of the team fanned out in search of other victims or survivors. Once removed, the remains of the two Air Force men, with the Dog Tags affixed to them, were moved to the center of the small perimeter set up by the team.

The main cabin area of JG-26 was nearby. There was another body in this portion of what was left of the helicopter. Ron believed this was the body of Sp4 Joe Kusick because of the radio parts and antenna from the PRC-25 Radio on the body. The body did not have Dog Tags. SOG Teams never wore Dog Tags in Laos. Ron, with the help of Brooke Bell, extricated Joe's remains and added them to the poncho containing the remains of the two Air Force men in the center of the perimeter.

All this work was being accomplished in misty rain and intermittent showers.

The ground party at the crash site saw two individuals watching them from a ridgeline. Thinking that they might be survivors, a squad started toward them; but their actions were suspicious and it was quickly determined that they were enemy soldiers.

Perhaps they were trying to lure our troops into an ambush…a typical NVA tactic. The squad returned to the crash site and the two enemy soldiers disappeared. It left no doubt that there were NVA about and they were monitoring our activities.

Ron was informed that Charlie and Lloyd had found another Air Force crewman's body at the bottom of a ravine in a fairly flat and open area. He was covered with brush. It was Larry Maysey, the para-jumper. He had probably been thrown from the Jolly Green when it was hit. They also found Bruce Baxter's body towards the top of the same ravine. Both bodies were downhill from the wreckage. The Covey that relieved Captain Kippenhan the night before, had reported seeing one person, on fire, running downhill from the crashed JG-26. That was probably Bruce Baxter.

When Captain Gerry Young, the Pilot of JG-26 was fleeing the crashed aircraft, he reported finding a grievously injured American downhill from the wreckage. He could hear NVA approaching. Although partially blinded by the fire that enveloped him in the helicopter, he covered the body with brush to conceal it from the NVA.

Ron and Rick Bayer joined Charlie Harper at the body at the top of the ravine. It was 38 meters downhill from the crash site, badly burned and entangled in jungle growth in a narrow ravine cut into a very steep part of the hill below the wreckage of JG-26. The body was lying face up and it was definitely MSG Bruce Baxter. Although all his clothing has burned off, except his white underwear and his white socks, his face was recognizable. Bruce always wore white socks as a preventative measure against foot fungus problems.

Extrication of Bruce Baxter's body was extremely difficult due to the weather, terrain, and condition of the body. The team at the crash site decided to lift the remains straight up with a helicopter rather than try to drag them out of the gully and up the hill. Rick Bayer and Ron Bock rigged Bruce Baxter's and Larry Maysey's bodies for extraction using some rappelling rope. The other remains were brought from the perimeter to the location of Baxter's and Maysey's remains so they could be lifted out also. Lifting them out would be less difficult and less damaging to them than dragging them up the steep, rain-slick hill.

There was confusion about how many remains had been recovered, the number of survivors rescued, and the total number of persons for whom we were searching. The Rescue/Recovery element continued to search the area for the next hour with no new contacts.

We believed that all souls were accounted for and that seemed to be the consensus at all levels of command. Although the Air Force had terminated its search and rescue activity, they were keeping helicopters on standby to come for the remains if the weather broke. The decision was finally made to stand down because the forecasters said the weather wouldn't break before nightfall. The Rescue/Recovery element began the climb up the steep, wet hillside to the perimeter at the crown of Hill 891. All remains that were recovered were left in the ravine for helicopter recovery when the weather cleared. Moving the remains up the hill would have been extremely difficult and probably would have taken several hours, even though the distance was only 300 yards or so. Weather and terrain conspired against us.

By lunch time, the Rescue/Recovery element had rejoined with our perimeter. We all took a break and dined on lo-cal meals of...nothing...and then set about expanding and refining the perimeter for the coming night defense. It was raining lightly, but steadily, so we made sure everyone filled their canteens.

A short time later, several "Bodes" began talking excitedly and pointing down the hill. SFC Hamilton was the first American to see them... a platoon of NVA (maybe 30 or more) walking single file from west to east along a trail at the bottom of the hill. He took the binoculars that were taken from the NVA body the day before and tried to get a better look.

"Look at that! There's a white guy leading them. He has a white Pith Helmet and a red beard"

I could see the Pith Helmet without using the binoculars. We had several recon teams report seeing a red-bearded Caucasian, perhaps a Russian Advisor, wearing a Pith Helmet. I thought he was a myth, but maybe he was real.

Lloyd was checking it out with the binoculars and agreed that he might be a Caucasian. We looked at a map. Lloyd plotted the NVA position on the map. The NVA were at least 1000 meters downhill from us.

Gilbert Hamilton set the bi-pod of an M-60 Machine Gun on a stump in the middle of our perimeter. I looked through the binoculars and told Hamilton that it is an impossible shot. It was beyond effective maximum range and downhill. He responded in his usual fashion, "Bull shit!"

He opened up with the M-60 as I watched through the binoculars. I was skeptical but ready to adjust his fire. I was amazed to see NVA falling, including the guy we think was the Russian. Dirt was kicking up along the column. I was in awe. I looked over at Gilbert and he had the M-60 pointing at the sky, launching bullets like the Machine Gun was a Mortar. This guy was Davy Crockett, Alvin York, and Houdini all in one. What shooting…and in the rain to boot!

On the other side of the perimeter, SSG Bell was doing the same with the other M-60. SFC Cavanaugh was bent over and Bell had mounted his machine gun on Cavanaugh's back so he could get enough elevation to engage the NVA. He was cheering as he shot.

I looked back at the NVA and some of them were running for the tree line, others were dragging dead and wounded, and some just stared at the top of the hill. I could only imagine what must be going through the minds of the NVA under attack. Bullets were falling on them from the thick clouds like lead raindrops. It took them many seconds to identify the source of the incoming Machine Gun rounds. The superstitious nature of their culture caused them to panic.

Actual combat is not like the movies. You don't hear the gun when it is fired at you. You hear the bullet as it passes by (hopefully). It makes a cracking sound caused by the projectile breaking the sound barrier. Then you might hear the sound of the gun firing, depending upon how far away the gun is. It may take several seconds for the sound of the shot to reach you. If there are many bullets being fired in your direction, which is commonly the case in modern combat, you may never hear the guns being fired because their sound will be overridden by the louder sound of the bullets. Often, you can get a sense of direction from the noise on the battlefield and individual firing positions can be located visually by the small puffs of smoke emitted from the gun barrels. Modern automatic weapons fire doesn't sound like movie gunfire either, it sounds more like popcorn popping (unless you are very close to it).

The NVA disappeared into the tree line.

SFC Hamilton had a little grin on his face. Only one in a thousand marksmen could make that shot. He and Brooke had definitely extracted some revenge for the men wrapped in a poncho a few hundred yards below us waiting for a ride home that would sadly never come.

I radioed Covey to get a "Sky Spot". There was no way that fighter-bombers could come through the clouds to deliver air-strikes in this weather but we might be able to get bombs on the suspected enemy position using radar bombing. Lloyd had the coordinates ready.

It was a time consuming process, so we made the request a "Prairie Fire Emergency" to speed things up. They were powerfully magic words, not to be used indiscriminately. Our request moved up to THE first priority for air support. Within fifteen minutes Covey radioed, "Bull Dog, get your heads down. You'll have bombs in thirty seconds!" We complied instantly. Normally "Sky Spots" were not authorized within 2000 meters of friendly personnel...and that's when the winds were much more predictable. However, the magic words "Prairie Fire Emergency" had over-ridden normal policies and the bombs had been released to strike a point about 1200 meters from us.

In about twenty seconds we heard a sound like a freight train coming and the bombs came whooshing out of the clouds to land right on the target. There was a huge secondary explosion and a large box-like object trailing smoke and fire came up from the trees and traveled about 400 meters east before landing and exploding in the jungle.

Faint sounds of the "spooked" and wounded drifted up to us from the bombed location. First they were hit by lead rain and now an aircraft they neither heard nor saw has bombed them. They are panicked! And I fear we may have poked the hornet's nest.

Lloyd's recollection:

"My recall of the sequence of events on that day is foggy at best. I know our main effort was to search the crash site and prepare the remains for extraction (Ron Bock handled most of that load and did a superb job).

Our other concern was getting the "Bodes" prepared to defend that hilltop against an NVA attack that we knew was most likely to come at any time. With the ceiling closed in we didn't have many options.

Gil Hamilton did engage that NVA column with the M-60 MG, placing accurate/effective fire on them and undoubtedly causing KIA/WIA to the NVA. Great shooting by a fine soldier.

I recall plotting an 8-digit grid coordinate of the NVA location that was relayed to Covey (probably by you) and I think it was sent as a Prairie Fire request. The fast mover dropped his load dead on the NVA location - great support by the AF."

The bombing results were radioed to Covey and we got back to work on our perimeter. Covey advised he would have to RTB but would be back before sundown to check on us.

Ron Bock adds one of his recollections:

"… After Ham laid in some rounds with the M-60, there was a lull in all activity, and it began to rain lightly. I took a squad and secured the west side of the perimeter. We moved carefully just into the tree line, not far from where "Ozzie" had stepped on the toe-popper the night before. I heard someone walking towards us from outside the perimeter. I alerted my squad to this with hand signals and we all peered into the woods from where the footsteps could be heard moving through the leaves. I saw what I believed was an enemy soldier and fired my M-16 twice on semi-auto. The person went down, and then my entire

squad opened up with full auto. The BAR man was to my left, and his empty shells ejected, hitting me on my left side. Whereupon, it sounded to me like the entire perimeter opened up with full auto, shooting at what I don't know. Just nerves, I guess.

Pretty soon, Ham came over, and I explained why I shot. Ham started to go into the tree line to check things out, but I cautioned him not to because that was the area where Baxter's team had put out the toe-poppers, so he decided stay back."

I shared Ron's memories of the brief "mad minute". The Cambodians didn't need much excuse to fire their weapons. Fortunately we got them to cease-fire in just a few seconds. We might need all the ammo we could get later. The little firepower demonstration had served to let our enemies know that we packed a punch and that we wouldn't be an easy victory for them.

It became quiet for a while and we used the time to strengthen our perimeter. The NCO's and I had been walking around the perimeter checking things out. I had left the radio propped against the same stump that SFC Hamilton used to elevate his Machine Gun a few hours ago. I looked over and saw him talking on the radio and I started in his direction. As I got closer, I over heard him say, "Fuck you, bitch!"

What now?

"Who are you talking to?"

"Some Russian bitch. She wants us to surrender."

Several days ago, one of the teams had reported hearing Russian being spoken on the radio. There is mounting evidence that the Communist advisors (Russians and Chinese) to the NVA are taking to the field, as the following excerpts from the previous week's weekly report from SOG to CINCPAC (Commander in Chief Pacific Forces) indicate.

> *PRAIRIE FIRE WEEKLY REPORTS (2 February - 29 Dec 1967)*
>
> *(The 1967 reports were discovered in Air Force History files at Maxwell AFB. No later reports have been discovered. Provided by Steve Sherman and RADIX Press. Transcription by Robert L. Noe.)*
>
> *PRAIRIE FIRE Weekly Reports prior to 2 Feb 67 NOT FOUND/SGS*
>
> *PRAIRIE FIRE WEEKLY REPORTS 162*
>
> *Air Force Historical Agency Declassified 4 Feb 93 SEA Declassification & Review Team*

TOP SECRET LIMDIS PRAIRIE FIRE

FROM: COMUSMACV (COURIER)

TO: CINCPAC (COURIER)

INFO: JCS (COURIER)

CINCUSARPAC (COURIER)

CINCPACAF (COURIER)

SOCPAC (COURIER)

TOP SECRET LIMDIS PRAIRIE FIRE JPCCO MACSOG 5625

Subj: PRAIRIE FIRE Weekly Report, 4 - 10 Nov 67 (U)

1. (TS) HIGHLIGHTS:

Excerpted from above described report:

g. Spike Team NORTH CAROLINA landed in the vicinity of DM— 4(XD724664) at XD715661 on 3OO918Z Oct 67. During the mission several groups of enemy personnel were heard speaking Chinese and Lao. The ST was extracted from the target area at XD708663 on 010115Z Oct 67. A heavy volume of AW fire was received during the extraction.

2. (TS) SUMMARY OF OPERATIONS:

a. ST IOWA landed in the vicinity of target CHARLIE-6 (YB509302) at YB506289 on 010720Z Nov 67. An estimated squad sized bivouac area was located by the ST. On 4 Nov the team monitored a radio transmission in Russian. On the same day the FAC directed TAC air strikes against personnel and equipment resulting in one secondary fire. The ST was extracted from the target area at YB475313 on 040815Z Nov 67.

As impressed as I was by Hamilton's usual eloquence, I was even more impressed by what he had just said.

"What? Give me that handset." I demanded.

"This is Bull Dog six. Who is this, over?"

A female voice speaking excellent, but accented, English responded, "This is Lieutenant Colonel (She gave an obvious Russian name, Lyudmila something or other), Advisor to the People's Army of Vietnam (PAVN-the name used by the NVA)."

I knew I should terminate the conversation immediately and switch to an alternate frequency, but I couldn't. This was just too unreal. I knew that the enemy was using direction-finding equipment to try and triangulate the source of my transmissions, but I was compelled to listen and respond for a few more seconds.

Lyudmila something or other continued, something to the effect that, "You are brave men and honorable warriors and there is no need for you to die. If you come to the bottom of the hill and surrender, you will not be harmed and will be treated with respect."

I couldn't help myself. Taking a page from SFC Hamilton's Book of Radio Procedures, I replied, "Fuck you, bitch. You come up here and surrender to us." Then I switched the radio to the alternate frequency and listened for a few moments to make sure the Russian wasn't on the alternate frequency as well. It seemed clear.

SFC Hamilton said, "See, I told you." While giving me one of his famous looks.

Apparently no one else had overheard us and no record of the Russian transmission exists today. SFC Hamilton died less than three months later of wounds received on January 17, 1968 when we were on another rescue/recovery mission. It is my word against the world regarding this conversation...but it happened.

I thought to myself, we must really be getting to them. I stayed there with the handset cradled on my shoulder so I wouldn't miss any attempt to contact us. It was obvious to me that something big was going on and that the NVA troops in the area were much better equipped and advised than what we'd been used to. I had been told that foreign advisors to the NVA did not venture out of North Vietnam. There was no one to relay this information to and no way to know if the transmission was monitored by the Army Security Agency (ASA) or any other intelligence gathering unit.

Sometime later we all heard the unmistakable sound of a mortar round leaving the tube somewhere to the west or southwest. We all dove for cover. Ron Bock threw his body over the Cambodian soldier who was wounded last night to protect him from the incoming mortar round. About ten seconds later there was a "crump" outside our perimeter to the northeast. The shot was long. A gray cloud of dust and smoke drifted westward from the explosion.

"Foop" another round was on the way. "Crump", still northeast, but closer. "Foop", "Crump" five more times. They were close but they hadn't got our range. Then it stopped. They had probably expended all the rounds they carried up the hill.

About an hour later, Covey came back. A panicked voice on the radio was saying, "Bull Dog, Bull Dog, this is Covey, over." Before I can answer, it comes again.

"Bull Dog, Bull Dog, this is Covey, Covey, on alternate, over."

I answered, "Covey, Bull Dog, go ahead."

"We've been calling and calling and finally switched to the alternate. What happened to you?"

I replied with the information about Lyudmila something or other and was met with the expected skepticism. I told them that other than a brief and ineffective mortar attack, things were relatively quiet. I advised that we would need another alternate frequency in case this one got compromised. I was told, "Stand by."

I could hear him relaying the information and request back to the Radio Room at Phu Bai. I could only hear Covey's side of the conversation, but it was easy to tell that there was skepticism and concern in the Radio Room at Phu Bai.

Covey got back to me with a new encoded alternate frequency and the information that the weather in our area should begin to break after dark. We were to be ready for extraction early tomorrow morning.

We again dined on nothing, although some of the "Bodes" had found some grubs in a couple of the old logs near the perimeter and were happily eating away. It was getting dark and we were getting ready for another long night. After the brief combat encounters this afternoon, we fully expected to receive a visit from the guys down the hill.

Bruce Luttrell slid into our hole and said, "Here sir, take this."

I asked, "What is it?" and he said, "It's a 'Green Hornet'. It'll help you stay awake."

I took it. It was a green and black capsule of Dexedrine.

As the last rays of the sun began to fade we thought we could see small patches of clear sky to the east. One more night and we could really think about getting off this hill. Lloyd and I discussed PZ options and how we would evacuate the remains of the brave men who died near here on the night of November 8/9. We would have to go back to the east for a good PZ, but first we would have go to the ravine leading down from the crash site to hook up the remains to a cable from one of the helicopters that would have to hover over the crash site. We could send a detail, with security, down first thing in the morning. It shouldn't take more than fifteen minutes to remove the remains once the "choppers" got there.

We got settled in and once again Lloyd and I took turns monitoring the radio and checking the perimeter. It was going to be a long night and I didn't think the "Green Hornet" was helping. I was really "on the nod".

The weather was clearing nicely and the clouds above us were shredding and thinning. It wouldn't be long before we were in the clear. "Blind Bat" checked in to tell us he was in the area and could be over us in minutes if we needed light. We advised the Bat that we would not call for flares unless we were in contact with the enemy, but we appreciated his presence and help. The drone of his far off engines served notice to the enemy that we were not alone and had help standing by.

A short time later "Alley Cat" came up on the radio. I could tell from the voice that it was the Airborne Battlefield Commander himself who was talking. He advised that they were lining up plenty of assets (aircraft) for the morning and that they would be getting us out at first light and for us not to worry. If we needed anything tonight he would personally see to it. It was obvious to me that this was not his first rodeo and he understood how lonely and helpless we were if something happened during the night. He checked in with us every hour or so. I appreciated it.

The night passed peacefully with only radio calls to interrupt the beautiful, star studded darkness. We were all grateful and surprised that we had not been in large-scale combat on this hillside. The greatest battle of the night for me was staying awake. The "Green Hornet" was highly over-rated in my opinion.

Eventually the sun rose and so did we. Tired, muddy, and cold, we waited for the first radio contact of the morning so we could relay our plans and get everything going. Lloyd put together a detail and returned to the crash site to hook up the remains. They started down the hill just before Covey arrived overhead.

Covey checked in and advised that the extraction force was airborne and should reach our location in about twenty minutes. I replied, "Negative. We need one H-34 with a hoist, a chase ship, and some gunship escorts to precede the lift ships by about thirty minutes. We need to lift out the remains."

Covey replied, "Negative on that. They want you out now! They do not want to hover any helicopters in this area. Orders are to move to a PZ for extraction, over." I could only hope that back in the rear they had information that made our immediate withdrawal necessary. We had not completed our mission.

I reiterated our concerns only to be told more forcefully that I would move the troops to a PZ post haste! I had no option but to call Lloyd and his group back. I wasn't leaving any living friendlies on this hill if I could help it. Covey then offered some A-1's for air strikes on any targets I had.

I advised Covey where our PZ was going to be and he directed a pair of A-1's with rockets, napalm, and cannons onto the tree line overlooking the PZ. I had Covey put the second pair of A-1's on the tree line where Ron shot the NVA soldier yesterday.

I put out a day-glow orange panel and requested the strike about 50 meters to the west of the panel. That's "danger close" for an air strike, but I had unshakable confidence in, and affection for the big, single engine, prop planes and the men who flew them. From an Infantryman's perspective, the A-1's, variously known to us as "Spads", "Hobos", or "Sandys", were undeniably the finest fixed wing close air support aircraft in the history of the world. It didn't hurt to have some of the most dedicated and courageous pilots in the Air Force holding their sticks either.

We violated one of the first rules of close air support. Never direct the aircraft directly over your position, but the terrain pretty well dictated how it would have to be done. The first Hobo came in from the east, directly over the perimeter at about one hundred feet and released two silver canisters of napalm.

His release point seemed well to our east and the cans of napalm tumbled lazily in his wake as he roared over our heads. The napes caught glints of morning sun making them sparkle a bit as they tumbled toward us in slow motion. It was going to be close, I thought. But it wasn't. The napalm hit the mark and sprayed its burning contents into the tree line. There was a "whoosh", the crackling of woods burning… and the enemy. Another pass by the wingman and we were ready to move out.

Ron's recollection:

"…you called in the napalm on that area, which was much appreciated, not only for the security it provided, but also for the heat it generated on that cold, misty morning."

We started toward the grassy area to our east. Lloyd caught up and he was not happy. "We didn't finish the mission," he said.

"I know, I don't have any choice. The birds were already inbound when they made the first radio call. They don't want to hover a helicopter down there and I can't say as I blame them. They just want us out as soon as possible."

We moved quickly to the pick-up zone. The helicopters arrived so fast we were a little disorganized on our exfiltration, but everyone knew the drill so we were gone in a matter of moments.

Ron put the wounded Cambodian on the first chopper. I got on the last chopper out, a Kingbee. We took a hit but it was anti-climactic. Everyone got back to Phu Bai in one piece. We had our steak and eggs. We were ravenous and some of us had two or three helpings. A quick debrief and we were told to "Hit the sack"...and then the "Green Hornet" kicked in and I couldn't go to sleep for the next eighteen hours. The next morning I was off to Saigon for a debriefing at MACV Headquarters.

The actual debriefing only took about four hours...just long enough for me to be called a liar. Apparently there were no Russian Advisors in Laos, there couldn't be a road where we saw the lights, and I was just a scared young Lieutenant trying to pass myself off as some kind of hero. I was never accused of failure but I knew.

I left the debriefing feeling as though my suspicions had been confirmed. This war, or police action, or insurgency, or whatever it was called was really screwed up. The guys calling the shots: President Johnson, Robert Mc Namara, and other high-ranking officials in the U.S, Government didn't have much of a clue what was really going on and they relied upon guys like the ones who had debriefed me for their information. The tactics being imposed on us by the military and diplomatic hierarchy were not designed to win but more to maintain the status quo. Not a great situation for those of us on "the edge of the wedge."

The debriefing in Saigon was scheduled to last a week. It was SOP (Standard Operating Procedure) for guys who had "crossed the fence". It allowed them time to unwind; but wallowing in one of the great "fleshpots" of Southeast Asia was not my "thing". I was back in Phu Bai a day later. I didn't feel much like being among strangers. I failed the mission. I realized again how lonely I really was.

X

At this point, about 2 months into my first tour, I had been "across the fence" twice and I'd patrolled locally. I'd seen the enemy and heard him talking and I had heard his screams. I had yet to fire a single shot in anger.

I'd also seen rain…lots of rain! Vietnam had two rainy, or monsoon, seasons. The Winter Monsoons occur in the north (from the Central Highlands of South Vietnam north and throughout North Vietnam) from October to March. The Summer Monsoons occur from late April to October and stay south of the Central Highlands in South Vietnam.

The two monsoon cycles were entirely different. In the south (Summer Monsoons), the rains came out of Cambodia at 4:03 P.M. You could set your watch by it. The rain was dark and looked like a curtain coming across the paddies. It rained really hard for a couple of hours and then it stopped. It didn't rain much at night down south.

In the north the rain set in for several days at a time. It was mostly a drizzle, but it never let up and it turned the ground into a quagmire. The clouds were thick and played havoc with our operations. The rain would stop for a couple of days and then start again.

The monsoons were essential to life in Vietnam because the growing of rice was so dependent upon the rain. Rice farming requires lots of water.

Rice is part of the reason that North Vietnam wanted to "liberate" (conquer) South Vietnam. The North is very mountainous and doesn't have much arable land. The North doesn't produce enough to feed its people. The southern part of South Vietnam is river delta and, except for the cities, it is all farm land. The South produced lots of rice!

When the rains came, the paddies would fill up with water and the next rice growing cycle would begin. On the numerous small farms, all the family members would participate in the rice planting. The paddies would be plowed, and otherwise prepared. Bundles of seed rice (small rice shoots saved from the previous harvest) would be delivered to each paddy by cart.

The young shoots of seed rice would then be spaced about six inches apart and pushed down in the mud by the women. The men would help after they had finished plowing and delivering the seed rice. Children who weren't school age tended the livestock, including the Water Buffalos. It was back-breaking work.

The Water Buffalo were important to the families and were used for anything that required power and strength. There were no tractors. The Buffaloes were very ill-tempered and dangerous, even to family members. (During my second tour, one of the Advisors to the RF/PF [like our National Guard] went around a hooch [house] during a night patrol and was charged by the family Buffalo. He was badly gored and almost died.)

The family Water Buffalo was tended by the youngest boy in the family. The little guys carried nothing but a switch. Once the buffalo was harnessed to a cart or plow, the older men took over, but the rest of the time, the little kids handled the giant beasts…and they didn't mess around. Very disciplined!

The rice grew quickly and it rained often. The color of the rice was gorgeous. As the rice grew, it pretty much took care of itself and the families turned their attention to raising other vegetables. Everything grew well. Families had large vegetable gardens. They kept what they needed and transported the rest to the towns and cities, sold it in the market places, and bought or bartered for the other things they needed.

As the rainy seasons tapered out, the grains of rice would emerge at the top of the plant (like wheat). The rice would typically be two to three feet high. The paddies would dry up and the rice plants would die.

The rice harvest would cause another flurry of activity. The now dried out rice would be cut off near ground level and gathered in sheaves. The sheaves would be beaten against the sides of large baskets; the rice would fall into the baskets, and the sheaves of rice straw would be saved to make mats, baskets, roofs, and walls. Nothing was wasted.

During the dry season, the mud turned to dust. The farmers spent that time fixing their hooches and equipment so they could start the cycle all over again. There were no vacations, no Disneyland, just the wet season and the dry season. The city folk fared a little better. At first it angered me that I was there fighting for them and many of them wouldn't take sides. I know now that they were just trying to survive. It wasn't their war; it was their government's war. They were good people and they worked hard. I wish we had been allowed to prevail because I think we, and the Vietnamese people, would be much better off today.

Although rice was the major agricultural endeavor, there were other crops being raised…rubber, sugar cane, and pineapples were grown for profit by companies big and small.

The villages of Khe Sanh and An Loc, where major battles took place, were originally rubber plantations. Even during the war, some rubber was being produced. In War Zones C and D near Saigon, many of the plantations had been abandoned. They were overgrown and dangerous. In the Central Highlands, there were still beautifully tended rubber groves. The abandoned groves were dangerous and dark.

The French operated huge rubber plantations (Michelin was the largest) in Vietnam.

West of Saigon, there were fields of Sugar Cane, though the production of sugar was greatly reduced by the fighting in the area. Processing was done by hand because the commercial cane processing plants had been shut down.

In the late 1800's South Vietnam was part of French Indochina, as was North Vietnam, Laos, and Cambodia. The entire area, which lay between China and India, was a Federation of French Colonies. It was heavily colonized by the French until WW2. The French influence was strong in French Indochina. Saigon (now called Ho Chi Minh City) was called the Paris of the orient. French was a common language.

The Japanese took most of the French Indochina territory during the Second World War. As soon as the Japanese surrendered, the French tried to reoccupy French Indochina but were immediately opposed by the Viet Minh, led by Ho Chi Minh. During the war, Japanese cruelty and a drought/famine took the lives of two million Vietnamese. The Viet Minh organized a relief effort and got the support of many who lived in the north.

Ho Chi Minh appealed to the U.S. for support to throw the French out, but because of our alliance with the French during the war, our President refused. Ho Chi Minh then turned to Russia and China for support, which they gladly provided.

The Viet Minh, with backing from various Communist countries, began a guerilla war against the French. It was low intensity at first, but eventually grew into a conventional conflict, mostly fought in the north. In late 1953, a French force of 1800 paratroopers parachuted into Dien Bien Phu in the northwestern part of the Democratic Republic of Vietnam and pushed the Viet Minh out. Dien Bien Phu sat astride a major supply route from what was then the Democratic Republic of Vietnam to Laos. The Viet Minh were supporting Communist troops in Laos called the Pathet Lao and the supply route was critical to the communist efforts in French Indochina.

General Vo Nguyen Giap, leader of the Viet Minh, quickly surrounded the French force and began moving heavy artillery into the hills around Dien Bien Phu. The winter monsoon was setting in and resupply became difficult for the French because of the weather. By spring, they were being relentlessly bombarded by Viet Minh artillery and ground assaults and were barely holding on. In mid-1954, the French withdrew (surrendered) and French Indochina was divided into the countries of Laos, Cambodia, North Vietnam, and South Vietnam by the Geneva Convention.

The Viet Minh troops that stayed behind in South Vietnam, reformed as the Viet Cong and began waging guerilla war against the south. Our assistance to South Vietnam grew slowly, until 1965, when we introduced conventional ground forces. Things escalated quickly from there.

XI

By mid-December, I had been in Vietnam for three months and I was feeling confident and secure in the knowledge that I could function as a leader in combat with the exceptional men assigned to SOG. But by this time I had developed little confidence in how the war was being waged. I was at the tactical end and had no clue about the big picture. I did not get a sense that there was a plan to achieve victory. Just rack up the body count to keep the press happy. It seemed to me that American soldiers were pawns in a diplomatic/political effort to maintain the status quo.

For our part, we operated in an extremely dangerous environment and took unbelievable chances to bring in intelligence about the enemy's plans, locations, and activities. As often as not, I think our information was disregarded.

SOG did not like to let the "Hatchet Forces" languish in camp for too long, so on December 14, 1967, Bill, Rod, and I, along with the NCO's from A-323 and some strap-hangers crammed the Red Devil Battalion on a C-130 and took off for Kontum.

The Air Force crew Chief/Load Master of the aircraft was enthusiastic and in preparation for take-off he was vaulting all over the inside of the aircraft setting switches and doing his other duties. We were all jammed in there pretty tight and it was hard to move around. I was sitting on the floor at the very front and when we started to taxi he strapped himself into a jump seat next to me.

He asked me if they were Montagnards (The tribal hill people usually associated with Special Forces). I explained that they were Cambodians. He remarked that they really looked mean and I told him they were just mad. "About what," he asked? "You", I answered. He was startled and I explained that the Cambodes were Buddhists and didn't like to be touched on the head or shoulders because it disturbed their personal invisible Buddha which rode on their heads or shoulders. Prior to taxiing, he had been steadying himself by putting his hands on their heads and shoulders as he moved around the aircraft. Kind of freaked him out! He went upstairs to the cockpit for the remainder of the flight.

We got to Kontum and got our troops settled in and then accompanied the FOB 2 Operations Officer out to the target area in a Huey from the 119th Aviation Company. The slicks went by the call-sign "Gators" and the gunships were "Crocs". We had an entire U.S. Army Aviation Company, plus Kingbees, to support this mission.

We got over the area late in the day. The Target Box was designated Hotel 9. Each FOB had its hotspots. Ours, at FOB 1, was Oscar 8. Hotel 9 was FOB 2's. The Target Boxes were usually 6 kilometers on a side. For the duration of the mission, no ordinance could be dropped in the target box unless under the direct control of the team or Covey. This target was in the tri-border area (where South Vietnam, Cambodia, and Laos meet). It was across the border from Dak To where vicious fighting had been occurring. Hotel 9 was where the NVA went to rest and re-equip. Hotel 9 was also called the "Golf Course" because it had an area with a large expanse of grass, like a golf course fairway bordered by a wide, shallow river on the east and north. The triple canopy forest that had been there was defoliated leaving lots of large, bald trees that were light grey colored. Lots of people were walking around when we got there, but they quickly disappeared. We stayed well away so as not to telegraph our interest and to avoid getting shot down in the process.

All our clever attempts to disguise our intentions were for naught. The FOB 2 guy had his head set on radio instead of intercom so everything he said was monitored by the enemy. Hotel 9 was a bad place and we were getting off to a bad start.

The next morning we transported the Red Devils to Dak To in a combination of "Gators" and Kingbees. The helicopters refueled and my platoon was the first to go in. SFC Bruce Luttrell was in the first Kingbee and I was in the second Kingbee. Bruce and I had agreed that if the LZ was hot, he would throw a red smoke and we would abort.

There were no prep fires planned because we were well beyond any artillery fan (areas covered by friendly artillery) and no fighters were "fragged" (scheduled) for the mission. We did have the four "Crocs" to start with and we may have had a pair of A-I's on stand-by because when the shit hit the fan, the A-I's got there really quickly.

As we were inbound to the target area in our trusty Kingbees I could see the sunlight sparkling on the river from about 10 miles out. It looked beautiful, as most of Southeast Asia does, but the war had done its damage. The beautiful green landscape was like a beautiful woman…with a bad case of acne (bomb and artillery craters). But enough mind wandering. It was time to focus. I knew this was going to be really messed up. We were sent to Kontum because FOB 2 had used up all its troops trying to get into Hotel 9. Our mission was the typical ambiguous, "Go in there and see what you can develop."

As we closed on the "Golf Course" we passed over a platoon of NVA on a road. Two gunships broke off to attack them. It was an ambush! The area erupted in gunfire and the first "Croc" was shot down and auto-rotated (a controlled crash) away from the area. The remaining two gunships that were to cover us peeled off to join the survivor of the first pair in a wagon wheel over the downed "Croc". Our Chase ship peeled off also to pick up the crew from the gunship that was shot down.

We continued in with no fire support and no chase ship in case one of our helicopters was shot down. I was now seeing extensive trench works and bunkers that must have been camouflaged yesterday when we were doing our reconnaissance. I also saw some NVA up in the defoliated trees. Everything I saw was oriented on our landing zone. Here we go again.

The first Kingbee landed without drawing fire, but as SFC Bruce Luttrell exited the aircraft with his small contingent of Cambodes, I started seeing enemy fire. There were two small grey puffs on the landing zone and two of the Cambodes went down. I was already on the radio calling out to abort the mission. The pilot looked back at me and I motioned him to go on. We were almost on the ground anyway and Bruce was going to need help.

We hit the ground with a bounce, and as I was scooting out, I heard a couple rounds hit the Kingbee. The popcorn sound was loud. Bruce and his guys were in a small bomb crater about 20 yards from where we touched down. One of my Cambodes went down, but his buddies were already dragging him to the crater. I slid into the crater and yelled at Bruce, "Hey, what happened to the red smoke?" He gave me one of those looks that Senior NCO's reserve especially for Junior Officers and said, "I was busy!" I gave him my best grin. At least we still had our senses of humor.

Bruce was organizing our return fire. Most of the enemy fire was coming from the tree line 20 meters to the north. I could see movement. I was on the radio with Covey declaring a "Prairie Fire Emergency". Then we heard the first mortar leaving a tube to our west and I reported that to Covey. The mortar shell landed in the middle of the LZ. I heard the mortar again. The shell landed closer. Covey informed us that he had 2 A-1's ("Hobos") standing by and I gave him my best estimate of where the mortar was.

While the first "Hobo" was setting up for his run on the mortar, I shot two NVA in the north tree line. One showed himself briefly as he crawled forward. I shot at the place where I thought he had crawled to and he rose up and then went down like he had been shot. The second guy crawled out to get him and I killed him.

I also reversed my Bush Hat so the orange panel I had sewn inside would show to the aircraft overhead. The Cambodes were very superstitious about my hat. They liked to look at it but didn't like to touch it because my brother, Barky, had sent me a rattlesnake skin which I made into a hatband for my Bush hat. The Cambodes thought snakes were "Numba 10"...bad juju!

The "Hobo" started his run on the mortar and a big anti-aircraft gun (probably a 20mm, maybe a 37mm) opened up from a ridge further to the west. The big A-1 pickled 2 napes (napalm) and got a hit on something because there was a good secondary explosion. However, the Hobo was hit and smoke was coming from the engine. He pulled off and his wingman, who had obviously spotted the anti-aircraft gun and adjusted his run, pickled 2 napes and silenced the gun. He pulled off and joined his lead to escort him to Pleiku (the nearest Air Force facility).

We had a lull in our fire support and the volume of enemy fire picked up. It got really dangerous to stick your head up over the edge of the bomb crater. The area around the crater was being plowed by bullets! Even though the ground was semi-moist, dirt was flying everywhere. I got a face full of dirt including in my eyes which stung a little because of the sweat pouring down my face. This must be the way Custer felt. The A-1's were gone. The gunships were gone. (A second gunship and the chase ship were damaged during the pick-up of the downed "Croc"). The two Kingbees that brought us in were gone to see how bad their battle damage was. It turned out to be negligible and they were back in the fight quickly. The rest of the helicopters were orbiting to the southeast, waiting to come in. That wasn't going to happen here today. My effort was now to put enough accurate air-strikes in the immediate area so it would be relatively safe for a couple of helicopters to come back in and get us out before we were wiped out. Fortunately, we had good weather, and after three months of depending on aerial fire support, I was pretty good at directing air-strikes.

In short time Covey was back on the radio with good news. Because of the "Prairie Fire Emergency", many fighter bombers were vectored to our location they were beginning to check in. The first fighters were Marine F-4's. They carried 250 pound bombs for an interdiction mission. Not the best armament for close air support, but I took what I could get. I told Covey I wanted 2 bombs in the tree line 20 meters north. Really close for iron bombs but I needed to suppress the closest enemy fire. Lead rolled in and nothing happened other than a lot of bad guys started shooting at him. He pulled off and Covey said he was coming around again. There had been some issues with new electronic bomb racks and his probably malfunctioned.

This time the bomb racks worked, but instead of 2 bombs, all the bombs left the racks. A voice on my radio was yelling to get down and I was yelling to everyone to cover their ears. Ka...blam! Blam! Blam! Blam! Blam! It was awesome. There were several seconds of stunned silence and then mud clods and tree limbs started raining down. The bombs were close but we had no injuries. My bush hat got blown off and was 10 meters away from our crater. "My" Cambodian soldier ran out and got it and brought it back to me, rattlesnake hatband and all, with a big smile on his face. Gotta love a guy like that.

About 60 meters of tree line was devastated. I ran two more sets of fighters getting more secondary explosions. Covey was also putting strikes on targets in other locations, including the downed "Croc". Hotel 9 was definitely a target rich environment. The firing died down and a bunch of NVA emerged from dust and devastation and bull rushed us. We cut most of them down. One guy made it to the edge of the bomb crater we were in and I drug him in and finished him off.

Two Kingbees came in at treetop level accompanied by the two remaining gunships, which had rearmed, refueled, and returned, shooting everything they had at everything but our little bomb crater. We had three wounded, but everyone else was in pretty good shape. We were gone in seconds. Crossing over the tree line I looked down on a few bodies lying in several zig-zag trenches and noticed some wooden platforms in the trees. The NVA, fearing our airpower, had withdrawn or gone into hiding. Our total time on the ground was probably under a half hour, but it seemed longer. We were lucky. Good weather and outstanding aerial fire support saved the day.

Back at Kontum, we grabbed some chow and had a short debriefing. I reported that I may have hit several NVA and killed one in the bomb crater. I couldn't add much else except it was a very dangerous area and we should probably bomb the shit out of it. Everyone agreed that the LZ must have been mined with some type of "toe popper". Despite all the fire we received, our wounded were injured in the feet and ankles when they got off the choppers.

The next morning we were at it again with slight revisions to account for the helicopters that were damaged or destroyed. This time Rod Hoepner took the lead group. I know little about his experience in Hotel 9 even though I spent all day on a grassy hillside next to the runway at Dak To listening to radio traffic coming in from Covey and other aircraft. We were keyed up to get back in there, but his experience was like mine. Once we got people on the ground the emphasis changed to getting them back out. He had a rough time, but got everyone out. He had casualties and at the end of the day the "Gators" and the "Crocs" had only one flyable helicopter out of the 13 they brought to the party. Rod earned a Silver Star for his work that day and I know it was well deserved.

Hotel 9 was definitely a change. I didn't get rained on and I fired a lot of rounds with some real effect on an enemy that I could see…and I didn't miss any meals!

I had killed a few of my fellow human beings which was totally forbidden by my Judeo-Christian up-bringing. A huge moral dilemma by anyone's standards. I don't know how anyone else handled it, but for me, it was war and the men I killed were merely targets without human qualities. Had I not shot them, they would have shot me without compulsion. The guy in the bomb crater certainly tried. I was glad I had prevailed but I did not feel any particular emotion about it.

Later, I would have occasion to search a few of the targets I killed and I remember one in particular. His ID card said he was a lieutenant and he was my age. While going through his pockets looking for maps and codes I found a picture of his girlfriend or wife and a letter from home. He was me in a different uniform and I was struck by the futility and inevitability of war. Nobody hates war more than a soldier.

I was awake for a long time that night thinking about the little blind date girl. If killing was what had to be done to protect my men and get me back to the little blind date girl, then I would kill without remorse.

XII

All the military services have units with reputations for "acquiring" various items that weren't part of their Table of Organization and Equipment, (TOE) i.e.: a medical unit would not be authorized a tank but would be authorized an ambulance, etc. If the medical unit needed a tank, they would have to acquire it. Comfort items were the targets of choice.

Special Forces units have always been recognized for their exceptional abilities in the area of re-appropriation, particularly of comfort items. Any SF unit worth its salt starts with a large beer/soda cooler and builds their camp around it. Acquiring re-appropriated items is called "scrounging", and FOB 1 scroungers were the best!

Because of our scroungers and our club, FOB 1 was a paradox. The missions were extremely dangerous, but our camp life was generally far better than most. Our food was exceptional for Army chow, we had jeeps to drive at a moment's notice, and our bunkers and defenses were strong (including a re-appropriated ARVN tank that we buried in the northwest corner of camp and used as a bunker). In addition, we slept on clean sheets, our uniforms were cleaned and pressed, and our boots were shined daily by our "Hootch Maids" who were paid for by our club.

The "Club" offered us a place to relax and guns and rank were left at the door. There were a few problems as you might expect. There were a fair share of alcoholics who were fantastic in the field but who relaxed way too much in camp. Although guns were not allowed in the club, arguments started in the club sometimes spilled over into the Company Streets. There were a few nights that felt like we were living in Tombstone or Dodge City. I would just roll off my bunk onto the floor and trust the sandbags to protect me if things got out of hand. Things usually de-escalated quickly.

The club also was a big draw to the Seabees and aviation units that supported our FOB and our missions. They spent lots of money at the club for drinks, snacks, and on the slot machines…and they were always up for a good trade.

Beside free maid service, we all benefitted in other ways from the club. It was a place to gather and drink of course, but the money made by the club provided for plaques, jackets, movies and, very occasionally, a floor show. If someone had to go home on emergency leave, or had an opportunity to take an extra Rest and Recuperation Leave (R&R), the club fund would give them money to cover some of the costs. (The Blackbirds had to fly to Taiwan to have their electronics maintained and up-graded each month or so. Frequently SOG Operators who had earned some extra time off went with them for an off-the-books R&R.)

Our "Room 2 Hootch Maid" was Co Vui Dung (pronounced Zung). Co meant young girl and Ba meant older or married woman. Most of the maids were Co's.

There was a senior maid who was a Ba. She took good care of her "Girls".

We decided Vui was about 16. We called her "Missy". She was very shy and, like most of the rural Vietnamese, very superstitious. Initially, she did not like having her picture taken. She did not understand cameras and thought that some of her "spirit" was being stolen each time her picture was taken. Later, as the maids began to know us, they relaxed. Being a maid for the Americans was a good job, and "Missy" Dung knew that to keep the job she had to be a hard worker and be scrupulously honest. As she got to know and trust us, she became intensely loyal and watched out for us and took good care of our stuff.

"Missy" Dung was not pretty by western standards; her face was very pock-marked from chicken pox or small pox, but she was a sweet girl. Just before the holiday season in 1967, I gave her some local money that I had. I had no use for it. It was a single bill with lots of zeros, maybe 100,000 piasters, I don't remember for sure. She started crying and tried to give it back to me. I convinced her that I wanted her to have it as a holiday present. The next day she brought me a beautifully wrapped package. It was a pair of cut glass cuff links. It was cheesy costume jewelry, but it's the thought that counts. The price tag was still on them ($9,000, but probably just a few dollars in U.S. currency). I, of course, made a big deal about it which pleased her. She was one of the many good people I met in Vietnam. I hope she survived the war and has a happy life.

When we were in camp, we always ate well. In addition to really good Mess Sergeants who were premier scroungers, we had a Vietnamese Chef who cooked for the French before us. We called him Papa-san and he had a room at the back of the kitchen. Rumor had it that the French sent him to cooking school in Paris. He ran a tight Vietnamese crew and put out some great chow. The Mess Sergeant was always scrounging and we had lots of fresh food.

We also had lots of jeeps that had been re-appropriated from the Marines. It was easy to pinch a jeep that was left unattended at the 3rd Marine Division Base down the road. We drove black jeeps with Vietnamese license plates as opposed to the olive drab jeeps of the Marines. We could drive a former "Marine" jeep in one end of the motor pool barn and have it emerge several hours later, painted black, covered in mud and small dents, and with a yellow Vietnamese plate. Special Forces Troops had a reputation for making off with anything they needed to make camp life better…plywood, air conditioners, forklifts, Conex containers of steaks… you get the picture. We fought hard, we lived well, and we made no apologies for it.

A lot of the scrounging was a result of some very successful enterprises run in one of the back rooms. As an example, one of the Ba's spent all day sewing North Vietnamese flags. The finished flags would be put near the Motor Pool where they could be run over by various vehicles. They would then be rinsed off and left to dry in the sun where they would receive cigarette burns and splashes of chicken blood from the Mess Hall. When they were judged to be authentic looking, the flags would be traded for a lot of the good stuff we enjoyed while in camp.

What we couldn't trade for, we took. Sometimes we even returned things when we were finished with them. It was all a big game and there were plenty of other units trying to run similar scams on us, but I think we always came out the winner. The game stopped when units were in real need. We supplied the Marines with a lot of needed equipment. Their stuff was old and worn out...we gave them all we could spare. The Marines were great guys and all of us had back channel contacts with our friends down the road. It wasn't unheard of to saddle up and go to the aid of local Marine units that needed help.

We also took good care of our Cambodian and Nung soldiers. We built a large open-air shower for them. Saturday became bath day and I think they really enjoyed it. One Saturday the cisterns went dry and the Cambodians went on strike, refusing to go on missions or training until there was enough water to bathe in. It was the dry season and it took several days to find, purify, and transport that much water, but by the next Saturday, things were back to normal and everyone was happy.

The Cambodian soldiers were wonderful people who came from a very hard existence. Once you gave them something (like showers) woe be unto you if you tried to take it away. We worked hard to make their lot in life better and they worked equally hard to serve us well. Trust and loyalty were everything between us.

I remember once when Bill was headed to the shower room and had forgotten to leave his watch in the room. Rather than go back, he put it on a post outside the shower room. When he came out to get it, it was gone. He mentioned it to Sam and a short time later the Cambodes hatched a plan to find the thief. They put another watch on another post and waited for the thief to take it. A withered old man who had been working in camp saw it and picked it up. He was immediately set upon by about two dozen enraged Cambodian mercenaries seeking street justice on Bill's behalf. We got things broken up before anyone got hurt, but it left the old man dazed and confused. The incident was a great example of their loyalty and simple thought processes.

Some of the most sublime times for me were just after dinner. We'd sit on the sandbag wall (to keep bullets and rocket or artillery fragments from going through our room) by our hooch and some of the Cambodes would come over. We would enjoy the sunset, Bill would smoke his pipe…we all enjoyed the smell…and we'd play mumbley peg with our knives, or we'd pitch pebbles (instead of pennies) or play horse shoes. We would all laugh and gamble on the games. It was carefree and the war went away for a few minutes every evening in camp.

The indigenous personnel had their own Mess Hall and we kept their kitchen well stocked. That required lots of rice…and rice meant rats. Supply and Mess Sergeants fought a constant battle against the rats and employed some unique abatement methods.

Toward the end of my time at FOB 1 somebody installed a Python in the Supply Shed. It was a large building containing tons of rice as well as other dry goods and supplies. The snake (Mr. No-shoulders) frequently hung out in the rafters during the day. When people came in for supplies, he would swing down from the rafters and check them out. It was unnerving to catch sight of the snake out of the corner of your eye and see the tongue flicking in and out. Mr. No Shoulders grew very large, very quickly and the rat population declined accordingly.

The Mess Sergeant took a different approach to his rat problem. The rats burrowed under the Mess Hall and one of the Mess Sergeants had the idea of pouring gas into the rat burrows to drive them out. He would then try to hit them with a baseball bat. He had minimal success, so the tactic escalated to setting fire to the gas around the entrance to the rat hole. This method was a little more labor intensive because of the danger of burning down the Mess Hall. The Mess Sergeant had a cook standing by with a bucket of water.

The gasoline soaked rats would emerge from their holes, catch fire, and start running with the bat wielding Mess Sergeant in hot pursuit. It was fun to watch and somewhat successful. The tactic ended one day when a flaming rat ran into an open ammo bunker. The Mess Sergeant reversed course in mid-air and ran the other way yelling, "Duck!" The rat expired and smoldered out without causing an explosion, but fire was discarded as a rat killing method.

The rest of us tried to do our part. A lot of us took our turn with the bat. At night, 1LT Vowell and Sergeant Parry chased rats with a Starlight Scope (Night-vision device) and a silenced 9mm Sten gun. Parry would spot the rats with the scope and direct Bill's fire. It was all fun and games until Bill went full-auto and shot up the Mess Hall one night. Papa San erupted from his room yelling all kinds of Vietnamese obscenities and threatened to quit if it ever happened again.

Another group tried to promote Friday night "Rat Races". Their plan was to capture some rats and race them around one of the graves inside our defensive perimeter.

We had several Buddhist graves inside our wire. They were quite nice as graves went. FOB 1 was close to the South China Sea so the water table was high, and the graves were built mostly above ground. The graves gave lots of protection in a firefight and we frequently set up in cemeteries when we were night-patrolling around camp. The graves would have made perfect raceways, but the project never really got off the ground. I think the schemers only caught one rat.

All in all, life in camp was good and our morale was high. Many of the air crews that supported us volunteered to come back because camp life was so good. Having air support that was familiar with our AO and methods of operations was a real help to us.

XIII

After our trip to the Golf Course, the pace of operations slowed a bit in anticipation of the holidays. For the past several months the teams, both Recon and Hatchet, from all the FOB's had been across the fence acting as canaries in the coal mine, only to return and have their hard won information ridiculed and disregarded by the intelligence types. It was frustrating, but we were the first to know something big was coming. We had already seen and felt it. We took lots of casualties and lost many long-time Special Forces Operators during the fall of 1967.

For now, Christmas was upon us and we were rewarded with a meal that rivaled anything the finest stateside hotel could offer. After Christmas dinner, Bill, Rod, and I had a few beers and wandered over to watch the Cambodes play volleyball. It wasn't long before we were challenged to a game. It was the three of us against about a dozen of them. I don't remember who won, probably the Cambodes, but I think we held our own. During a break in the action, Rod, who was a dedicated weight lifter, grabbed Bill around the knees and lifted him up, lost his balance, and dropped Bill on his head. When Bill's head hit the concrete it sounded like a watermelon had been dropped out of a second story window. I thought he was dead. When I got to him, he gave me one of his lop-sided grins, got up and started another game of volleyball. He had a granddaddy of a headache the next day. He attributed it to drinking too much beer on Christmas Day. I guess, in a way, he was right.

Bill was a pipe smoker. He smoked his pipe every night in camp after dinner and it always mellowed our mood. It smelled so good. He gave me a nice pipe for Christmas with some good tobacco. It greatly enhanced my after dinner relaxation. We enjoyed our evenings sitting on our sandbags and mingling with our Cambodian soldiers. I smoked it for about a year and a half off and on before it was run over by a fire truck and destroyed. But that's another story.

We coasted through the next week and started gearing up for more missions after the first of the calendar year. The operational tempo picked up fast and teams were having a hard time getting into their AO's across the fence. The weather was bad and the NVA was everywhere. The bell rang for me again on January 14, 1968.

On January 12, 1968, Recon Team Indiana inserted into Laos about 18 to 20 miles south of Khe Sanh. The area was heavily vegetated with single canopy jungle and thick, sharp elephant grass. Late in the day, the team was ambushed. They broke contact and set up a defensive perimeter on a small hill, however, in the confusion, two Nungs and SSG James Cohron, the Assistant Team Leader, were separated. The team was unable to locate Cohron or the Nungs and called for extraction.

We were tasked with the Bright Light mission. In addition to the usual load out, we were equipped with some experimental squad radios that worked on line-of-sight. The radios consisted of a small hand held transmitter and a receiver that clipped to your hat near your ear.

On the morning of the 14th we departed Phu Bai for Khe Sanh in USMC H-34's with a force of 36 (6 US and 30 Cambodian). We landed at Khe Sanh and Top Fisher and I went to the FOB 3 TOC to coordinate the mission with the Khe Sanh launch team (LT. Ed Havens and MSG Billy Waugh). I got the bad news that there were several other teams in Laos who would share our air assets which consisted of maybe 8 Marine H-34's. No other air support was fragged for January 14, other than a Covey on stand-by. No A-I's, no gunships...bare minimum support.

The Marine H-34's had refueled and we had our maps and SOI's, so we were good to go by mid-morning.

After a short 20 to 30 minute flight, we landed in the middle of a relatively flat plateau. The elephant grass on top of the plateau was 10 or 12 feet high and thick. In some spots it was so thick that the point man would have to throw himself up on the grass and fall to the ground to make a path. Our movement was slow and noisy. We couldn't see anything because of the grass. The area we were interested in was 500 meters to our south. Moving through the Elephant Grass was exceedingly slow and dangerous.

We worked our way south to a little hill top at the south end of the plateau where Indiana had had their defensive perimeter. The hill reminded me of "Little

Round Top" on the Gettysburg Battlefield in Pennsylvania. We found the ambush site nearby in medium thick bamboo. There was some blood splatter and shredded vegetation, obviously from gunfire, but not as much as we expected. There were several places where grenades had detonated, but not much evidence of fragmentation. We felt as though the ambush may have been a deliberate effort on the part of the NVA to take prisoners. We followed drag marks and blood trails for 20 meters or so but they petered out. I had 3-man teams do cloverleaf searches out in all directions, but they didn't find anything. Cloverleaf was a method of checking the immediate vicinity quickly. In this case four teams went in four compass directions about 100 meters, moved to their right 100 meters, and then came back to the start point. Nothing was found so we moved off the hilltop and back into the grass and started down the west side of the plateau following the path that RT Indiana had taken after leaving the hilltop. We were looking for any sign of the three missing RT Indiana members.

We moved back to the northwest part of the plateau where there was plenty of room for an extraction. The grass was lower and we could see across the plateau. We were in an area of saplings with larger logs on the ground from fallen trees. The logs gave us good cover and we had some concealment. I wanted to keep the team on top of the plateau because it was a good landing zone. I radioed our launch team in Khe Sanh that we had had negative results on our search for the missing men. I was told to sit tight because the H-34's were tied up pulling out another team in another part of Laos.

I was worried that we had picked up trackers, so SFC Gilbert Hamilton, Sp5 Gary Spann, and four indigenous troops volunteered to check our back trail. They got out about 30 meters in the tall grass and ran into heavy fire. Thanks to the experimental radios they were able to communicate. Everyone was hit. Hamilton was hit in the abdomen, Spann in the jaw, 2 indigenous KIA and 2 wounded. Hamilton was calling for help and began to pass out. Spann tried to take over but we couldn't understand him because of his wounds. In the meantime we came under fire from an RPD (Russian-made Machine Gun) and several AK-47's. We took cover behind some big logs and I remember I was lying in ants. I marveled at their strength and discipline. Despite the chaos around them they held a steady line and carried pieces of vegetation that were three times their size.

Hamilton came back up on the radio and it was the most pitiful sound I have ever heard. "Help us!" I couldn't stand it and told Top Fisher I was going to get him. I started over the log and a strong arm grabbed me by the back of my belt and yanked me back. About two seconds later the NVA machine gunner turned the top of the log into a thousand toothpicks! Fisher said the one thing that would make me stay, "That's not your job, sir. Your job is to lead us." He was right and I quickly came up with a plan.

SFC Hamilton regained enough consciousness to communicate and comply with my request to pop a smoke. As I recall, he tossed out a yellow smoke. I had the interpreter tell all the Cambodes with us that on the count of three we were all going to stand up and walk toward the smoke firing semi-auto from the hip... and not to fire directly at the smoke because that's where our guys were. It worked and we reached our guys in a couple of minutes. Naturally, I was calling for support and I was told to stand-by. Then I was told Covey was launching from Khe Sanh.

We got to our guys and secured the area. There were two wounded NVA in our new perimeter with brand new equipment (this was just prior to the siege of Khe Sanh). Their brand new AK-47's, with collapsible stocks still had Cosmoline packing and preservative grease in them. We had suppressed almost all enemy fire and a squad followed a blood trail out about 20 meters until I called them back. In the meantime one of the Cambodes killed the two prisoners. (One of our Cambodian KIA's was his best friend.) I really wanted the prisoners and probably should have had one of the Special Forces guys guard them, but we were all a little busy. I checked back with Khe Sanh to get an ETA on Covey and was told to stand-by. We were in a pickle. The longer we remained where we were, the greater the chances of a larger NVA force arriving to engage us. Covey never showed up.

I learned later that Covey had taken off from Khe Sanh and had been shot down, or crashed, immediately after take-off, killing the pilot, Captain Sam

Beach and Covey-rider, SFC Don Chaney, both great guys and a real loss for all of us. That explained why I wasn't getting any help.

We hadn't received any fire since reaching Hamilton's and Spann's location and I was hoping to get off the plateau before the NVA got more troops into the area. Given the initial volume of fire, I felt like we were facing 9 to 12 enemy and their probable intention was to set-up an ambush for any helicopters that would come for us.

In what seemed like 30 minutes, the Marine H-34's appeared. We popped smoke and I cautioned them that the NVA had retreated down the west tree line and they had an RPD. Ignoring our input as usual the first H-34 paralleled the tree line and got shot up pretty badly, probably by the RPD. It pulled off and headed back to Khe Sanh. I heard the crew chief was killed. There was no way for us to suppress enemy fire other than to shoot into the tree line. So we lined up a bunch of our guys and had them shoot up the tree line which they did with great gusto and it seemed to have the desired effect. The rest of the H-34's adjusted their approach and kept coming.

We loaded our dead and wounded on the first helicopter and I watched it struggle into the air. The second bird took out a half dozen Cambodes. The next several took out as many as they could. Then the last bird landed and we still had 7or 8 guys in the zone. We all got aboard and the H-34 bounced a few times but couldn't get airborne. We were too heavy to take off, which was a common problem at that density/altitude.

I could see the crew chief talking on intercom and I knew what was going to happen next. Sure enough, the next thing I knew he was pushing one of the Cambodian soldiers off. I jumped off also, because I was sure that they would not come back for one little Cambodian out in Indian Country and those were my guys on the chopper and I needed to get them out of there. Unfortunately, I left my pack, with the radio, on the H-34 so I was without any communication, but I still had plenty of ammo and some water.

After a few bounces, the last bird got away, and things got really quiet. We started crawling to the east side of the plateau trying to stay silent and we could hear the NVA talking. It sounded like they were lining up to beat the grass just like a big game hunt. That was a typical move for them. They usually did a good job of cleansing a battlefield. Things were going well until we crawled up on 2 of them and had to fire. I killed them both.

We withdrew the way we came throwing grenades at noises in the grass. We were rewarded on several occasions with screams or grunts. We were shot at as well, but we hugged the ground and the elephant grass protected us. Most return fire seemed high.

The clouds were low and broken and I heard helicopters. They were Jolly Greens. I flashed them with my mirror but they didn't see it and continued on. I reminded myself to keep the last grenade for personal use. I did not want to be captured!

We eventually got back to our original starting point and were getting ready to go down the side of the plateau because there was no place else to go, when we heard an H-34 coming back. For the second time that day, MSG Fisher had saved my life. When he saw me get off, he made straight for the cockpit to convince the Marines that they would be coming back to get me and my Cambodian side-kick. There were several versions of the story, one involved a weapon. Years later, Lloyd Fisher admitted to me that he had interceded on my behalf. When I asked him if he had threatened anyone with his weapon, he just said, "I took care of it."

I didn't want to take my eyes off the returning H-34, so I didn't see much else. I popped a smoke and started blazing away full auto into the grass. The helicopter roared in right on top of us. We dove through the door of the helicopter and "got the heck out of Dodge".

I remember the Crew Chief lit a c-ration cigarette and handed it to me. I didn't smoke cigarettes, but I took it and smoked the whole thing. Maybe that's what freedom tastes like. I have never smoked another cigarette since because I don't think any other cigarette in the world could ever taste as good as that dried up old c-ration "Lucky Strike".

The only thing I remember about getting back to Khe Sanh was that as we were landing, another Marine chopper was coming in from one of the outposts in the hills to the north where vicious fighting was taking place. A couple of medics were standing by to meet it and called for help. I ran over and they were wrestling a big blonde kid who had just had enough. He was growling like an animal and the look in his eyes told the whole story…combat fatigue. It took at least 4 of us to subdue him enough so the medic could give him a shot. I felt really bad for him.

I don't remember much about the next few days, but I'll always remember how alone I felt and I have always regretted that several airmen, several Cambodian soldiers, and several SF guys died in the engagement. SFC Hamilton later died of his wounds. If he hadn't volunteered to check our back trail things might have been much worse for us.

Gilbert Hamilton, a brave and dedicated Special Forces operative, was the only American soldier to die under my direct command in two tours of combat duty. He was a hero in every sense of the word. Gary Spann survived his wounds, but none of us ever heard from him again. He too was a dedicated and courageous Special Forces soldier. I wish that day had turned out better!

SFC Hamilton earned a Purple Heart and a Distinguished Service Cross (the second highest valor award that could be bestowed upon a U.S. Army soldier) and Sp5 Spann received a Purple Heart and a Silver Star for their actions on that day. I was proud and sad to write their citations.

So far, my "lessons learned" list had:

Lighten your load.

Don't wear underwear.

Lighten your load.

Put 18 rounds in a 20 round magazine.

Lighten your load.

Take more water.

Lighten your load.

Always take an extra can of peaches

Lighten your load.

Don't let your radio out of your sight.

XIX

The Marine Base and FOB 4, at Khe Sanh in the far northwest corner of South Vietnam came under siege on January 21, less than a week after we had been there. We were back in Khe Sanh a week later standing by to launch a mission that never went because of weather. Everybody was living underground. It made going to the latrine fairly dicey. You'd start for the latrine and hear a couple of rounds, usually mortars, being fired then you had a decision to make: how badly do you need to go? A real effort was made to maintain field hygiene in the trenches but eventually they got pretty nasty. I saw a latrine get hit by a rocket (NOBODY IN IT). There was toilet paper and stuff everywhere. Thankfully the rain helped it disappear in a few days.

Fortunately we were only there for a few days and I felt badly for the guys assigned there. Conditions were terrible at best. The weather was horrible and the mud was worse. There was a lot of incoming artillery and mortar fire. It was the start of something big, but we had seen so many NVA troops coming into South Vietnam in the preceding months that most of us thought there must be more to come. There was…

A couple of weeks before Tet, the Cambodes brought a skinny old cow into their area and staked her outside one of the latrines where a little bit of grass was growing. They brought her water and hay every day and I didn't think much about it. One morning a few days before Tet I looked through the screen at the front of the room and saw a bunch of Cambodes slaughtering the cow. Still didn't think much about it. I figured they were going to have a BBQ.

That afternoon a young Cambodian soldier, in a starched and pressed uniform with his hair dark and shiny from a liberal application of pomade, knocked on our door. He shyly presented Bill and me with invitations to a banquet that evening. We and Rod, along with members of A-323 showed up at the appointed hour and were seated on floor mats at a low "U" shaped table.

I confess that I don't remember much after that. I think it started with the local beer, Ba Mui Ba (Beer 33), which was rumored to have as much as 30% formaldehyde. We were challenged to drinking games by many of our soldiers and, of course, it got drunk out fairly quickly. I did my best to excuse myself so I could pour the nasty stuff out but I couldn't avoid it all together. I think we switched to rice wine when the food came. I was 22 years old and a typical "Ugly American". The Cambodians were honoring us and I didn't want to offend them, but the food was pretty unappealing to a guy who grew up on meat, beans and potatoes. I remember a bowl of carrots that looked like something I could handle. I ate a few carrots and discovered that underneath them were a bunch of chicken claws. That's about all I remember. I have no idea how I got back to my room or what I did the next day.

Sometime in mid-January, Captain Trujillo, the S-2 (Intelligence) officer, set up an easel and map of the Ho Chi Minh trail and South Vietnam in the middle of our FOB. All the Americans in camp attended his briefing. He proceeded to tell us about massive enemy build ups of men and supplies along the trail and that we should anticipate a large enemy offensive in the near future. This was not news to us! We had been witnessing the build-ups for the past several months. We had suffered casualties and deaths bringing information to our higher-ups regarding this. This was no surprise.

January 30, 1968, at midnight was the beginning of Tet. Tet is the Southeast Asian New Year. In that part of the world, the Buddhist Calendar is based on lunar (moon) cycles so the New Year falls on different dates. Both the North Vietnamese and the South Vietnamese had announced a 72-hour truce for Tet 1968, which had been the custom for several years. We all knew something big was afoot and we were ready, but I thought the North Vietnamese wouldn't make their move until after Tet. I anticipated a restful night.

I was wrong! At 3 AM on the 31st of January, the Viet Cong and the NVA launched attacks against Saigon, the Capital of South Vietnam, and 64 District Capitals. They also fired rockets and mortars at most allied airfields and a number of U.S. bases, including Phu Bai.

We were in the middle of the Northern Monsoon at FOB 1 and it had been raining off and on for a few days. The morning of January 31, in northern South Vietnam, was very wet and foggy. The cloud ceiling was about 25 or 30 feet up. Yet I awoke to the sound of helicopters spooling up.

I rolled out of my rack with the distinct feeling that something was drastically wrong. I grabbed my weapon and my "Bug-Out-Bag" (everybody's Bug-Out-Bag was different but each contained enough emergency survival gear to last a few days without support) and headed to the Tactical Operations Center to find out what was going on. The answer was the 1968 Tet Offensive.

We spent the day loading helicopters with boxes of ammo, medical supplies, fresh water, and anything else needed by the American advisors who were in a compound on the south side of the Perfume River outside Hue. Our choppers brought back many wounded. I don't recall hearing or seeing any other helicopters in the area that first day. The flying conditions were terrible and visibility didn't improve much during the day. The helos were getting shot at with great regularity but they never shut down until it got too dark to operate effectively.

A number of guys just got their stuff and boarded the helos during the day and flew to help with the fighting and we sent several of our medics to help with the wounded. Nobody asked permission or got clearance, they just rushed to the sound of guns to help anyway they could. They will always be my brothers.

The next morning as soon as it was light, a platoon of USMC tanks followed by a company of Marines passed by FOB 1 with the obvious mission of clearing Highway 1 between Phu Bai and Hue. The weather was somewhat better and there was more aviation activity. Everybody was getting busy. We spent the day strengthening our defenses and getting a grip on things. About sunset, the tanks and Marines came back by camp. It was obvious they had been fighting most of the day. They had lost 2 tanks and their numbers were smaller. It had been tough duty. The next morning they headed up the road again, only this time the infantry was in front of the armor. The Marines had plenty of "Grunts" but not very many tanks. The fighting lasted weeks.

At FOB 1 everybody was on standby for everything. While Commanders at all levels tried to come to grips with what was going on we were not at all surprised. We had been reporting significant traffic and build-up along the Ho Chi Minh Trail for the last several months. Obviously our hard-won information had been mostly disregarded. It made us furious to think that we had invested so much effort and lost so many killed or wounded for nothing. I rapidly became disenchanted with the Intelligence Services of both the military and the CIA.

The news was reporting shock and surprise and that Allied units all over South Vietnam had been caught unaware. Tet was being billed as a victory for the NVA and an embarrassing loss for the U.S. Nothing could have been further from the truth. It was a military and psychological disaster for the NVA and Viet Cong, but I digress.

Things got back to normal quickly and we began to launch missions again. At some point during the chaos, Maj. Snell called me to the TOC and offered me the job of Assistant S-3. (Staff jobs were designated as S-1 Personnel, S-2 Intelligence, S-3 Operations, and S-4 Logistics). I would stand in for the Operations Officer in his absence, but mostly I would be a Covey rider.

Things started fast. The next morning Covey was in-bound at first light. I met Captain Bart Switzer, call sign Covey 263, in the TOC over a cup of coffee and was told we would be surveying the area west of Hue. We would be looking for signs of a POW camp that supposedly held ARVN and civilian prisoners captured in Hue. There was also information about a group of German Red Cross nurses who were being moved from Hue to the Ashau Valley by the NVA.

One of the Operations NCO's drove us back to the airstrip where I got my first close up look at the O (for observation) -2. It was the militarized version of the civilian Cessna Skymaster. It had an engine on the front which pulled and an engine on the back which pushed. We called it the "blowsucker." It had many radio upgrades and Plexiglas inserts in the doors and ceiling to improve observation. The military version was heavier than the civilian version and could not fly on one engine. A single engine could extend the glide path a great distance, but there was no ability to gain altitude if we lost an engine.

Off we went into the wild blue yonder. I was excited! I had always wanted to be a pilot but never would be because of my color vision. This was as close as I could get and Bart was a cool guy who explained that he wanted me to be able to fly the Cessna in case something happened to him. With that he gave me a heading and the controls and I was flying! When we got to the area west of Hue he took control back and we began an hour of lazy circles and S's, looking for anything that might signal enemy activity. Eventually we turned our attention to Highway 547, running west from Hue toward the Ashau Valley. In most cases, the highways I mention were single lane dirt tracks.

It wasn't long before Bart said, "Hey, Look at that!" He yawed the airplane a bit so I could see down the road. It took a few seconds but then I saw a little dust coming up from the road and determined that it was raised by about 20 to 30 enemy soldiers walking westbound. Bart turned eastward and started gaining altitude. At 3500 feet he leveled off and turned back toward the west, aligning with the road. He throttled back and said, "Watch this!" It was about 1100 hours and the sun was at our back. He started a shallow, noiseless dive toward the unsuspecting enemy. A classic air attack.

We glided down to about 300 feet and Bart pulled the trigger that would send white phosphorous rockets swooshing from the rocket tubes on the wings. Nothing but a "click!" We gave each other a wide-eyed look and he firewalled the throttles. I looked at the rocket tube on my side and saw the bright red safety streamer that had "REMOVE BEFORE FLIGHT" stenciled on it blowing freely in the slip stream. OOOOPs! The NVA were disciplined and immediately formed on the road and barrage fired their weapons (everyone firing at a point in the sky that the plane must fly through). Fortunately we didn't seem to have any serious hits.

Bart was on the radio trying to get some fighters while I kept an eye on the NVA. They kept moving westward but stayed off the road. He said we might get some fighters in 30 minutes. 30 minutes came and went with no fighters. We were told another 30 minutes. The calls for air support in the days just after Tet were overwhelming and many went unanswered.

I really had to pee. The O-2 was too small for any moving around and did not have any facilities anyway. Bart gave me his yellow topped canteen. Ahhh, relief. Note to self: never drink from a yellow topped canteen.

Eventually Bart said we had to go or we would run out of gas and we departed toward Phu Bai. About half way there he asked me if I had anything I could throw out to lighten the airplane.

"You're kidding, right?" He said no. We finally had the airfield in sight and then the engines made a few coughs and chugs a couple times and the props stopped turning. It got really quiet, but Bart said he thought we could make it. I was watching the 4 strand boundary fence get closer and Bart said that if we cleared the fence we'd be home free. We made it by a couple of feet! We landed in the dirt and weeds of the runway overrun and came to a stop about thirty feet from the end of the runway. We got out and started pushing. Eventually a little tractor came out and towed us the rest of the way in. Pretty exciting first day I'd say!

During the several weeks just after Tet, the area received many rocket attacks. Most were aimed at the 3rd Marine Division Headquarters but FOB 1 and the adjacent ARVIN Training Center got a share of the incoming fire. We probably were hit by ten or twelve 107mm and 122mm Soviet made Katyusha Rockets. They packed a punch.

Since most of us kept containers of gasoline in our living quarters as a solvent for cleaning weapons, we had fire. Lots of fire! The Recon Team Rooms burnt to the ground, the Cambodian barracks burnt to the ground. We had no hoses or water pressure for fighting fires.

At one point we were worried that the mess hall would burn. I was in there with Staff Sergeant Anderson trying to put the fire out and there was a large explosion from a fully involved team room adjacent to the mess hall. Anderson went down and I had to drag him out through the tables and chairs which were scattered like pick up sticks. The air was getting a little smoky and I yelled for a little help. We were able to knock down the fire and save the mess hall. There were several other explosions and I was hit by debris but other than burning hair which I beat out immediately, I came through in great shape.

The Club Sergeant's quarters burned along with the 5 o'clock monkey. We all made a desperate effort to save it by setting up a beer can brigade and throwing beer on the fire pretty much to no avail. Several other quarters burned as well. We were able to save the club but our beer supply for the month had suffered serious depletion.

After dinner that night the Major took me aside and ordered me to write up Bronze Stars with "V" awards for him and the Operations Officer. I tried to beg off but he ordered me to do it and tried to sweeten the deal by saying, "Put yourself in for one too." I wrote them up but did not write myself up. I felt really sleazy. This was not what I thought the Officer's Corps was all about. I believed in honor and integrity. This was not honorable, even though I was ordered to do it. This would not be my only experience with this sort of thing.

Although U.S. and South Vietnamese forces sustained heavy losses during Tet, the NVA and Viet Cong were repelled from every location they had attacked or briefly held. It was a huge military loss for the North.

During this period, we began receiving new blood. We got 5 or 6 new radio operators fresh out of school as well as other individuals for various staff functions. They were the new generation. Longer hair, bandanas around their heads. They looked more like hippies than soldiers. I smelled marijuana in our compound for the first time. That was taken care of quickly. We also got some officers who were not Special Forces qualified. They filled some of the staff jobs. There was one guy who had a lot of attitude. He shall remain nameless. One night he got drunk and went out the back of the club to take a leak.

We had a very nice latrine set up behind the club. The urinal part was a two or three piss tube set up surrounded by a chest high wall. To enter you had to negotiate a little left, right, left maze. The LT. went out in the dark without a flashlight and negotiated the maze just fine, did his business, but couldn't find his way out. Ever a problem solver, he kicked his way out.

The next morning about 0700, I was heading to the Mess Hall for breakfast and heard pounding. I thought it was a little early for construction work so I drifted in that direction to see what was going on. I went behind the club and saw a very hung over LT. Attitude repairing the urinal supervised by a none too happy major, feet shoulder width apart and arms crossed over his chest. Attitude was gone the next day and I hope he learned from the experience. If he didn't find some humility he was not going to make it.

Another new lieutenant moved into the empty space in our room. He was definitely not SF but was a really good guy. For the life of me, I can't remember his name. He went down to the village within a day or two of arriving at FOB 1 and came back with a Buddha charm which he wore around his neck. It was the size of a silver dollar; a little gaudy for my taste. He was sure it was ivory and that he got a really good deal. I was sure it was plastic and he got taken.

We were still receiving some rocket fire and several days later we were working in the compound and I heard one coming in. Generally when you hear them it is only a few seconds before impact. I yelled, "Incoming!" and dove behind some sandbags. He stood there not sure what to do (it was his first rocket). The damn thing hit about 30 feet from him and he went down. I ran to him as he was trying to sit up. I started checking him out for wounds. He was gasping for air and I was sure he had a sucking chest wound, but I could find no wound and no blood. What I did find was his brand new Buddha broken into three or four pieces. It had stopped a piece of shrapnel that surely would have severely injured him.

I went into the village the next day and purchased my own Buddha charm. You can never be too careful. It wasn't nearly as flamboyant as the "ivory" charm. It was small and green and about the size of a quarter. I told everyone that it was real jade and that I got a good deal, but I knew it was plastic and I got ripped off. It didn't matter as long as it deflected lead when the time came.

After Tet the pace of operations just kept increasing. I flew every day, sometimes as much as eighteen hours. I particularly remember LT. Don Doll, who took my place with the Cambodians. His Hatchet Force was surrounded on a small hilltop on the Laotian side of the Ashau Valley. I was over him all day with two different pilots in two different airplanes. We finally recovered at Da Nang at about midnight.

I got a couple hours sleep and then went to the flight line kitchen to grab a bite of reconstituted eggs and soggy toast. I needed to eat because I knew I would be flying all morning, but it was disgusting. And then I drank two, not warm but hot, beers just to be one of the boys. It was awful and I knew I would probably be sick and I was. I spewed the meager contents of my stomach over the west side of the Ashau Valley about

4 AM. Believe me that was a move that impressed no one. My hope was that an NVA Officer was looking up at the sky that moment and got a face full.

Don was surrounded and needed help. The good news bad news was that the genius in Washington had decided by some twisted political logic that if we didn't bomb North Vietnam they would come to the Peace Table. He called for a bombing halt up north. As a result, NVA men and supplies came pouring down the trail. On the other side of that coin, plenty of bombing and attack aircraft became available for close air support missions.

The first aircraft to show up in support of LT. Doll were F-105's. They were customarily used to bomb the north. Day after day they flew into the most heavily defended airspace in history. The pilots were fearless, but they had little experience in dropping ordinance super close to friendly troops.

The NVA had learned to move as close to our guys as possible in an effort to negate the effectiveness of American artillery and airstrikes. We all tried to minimize casualties caused by friendly fire and had restrictions pertaining to how close artillery and bombs could be called in . . . except SOG. Most of us were comfortable calling the A-1's and helicopter gunships to within 20 yards. We were a little more cautious with the fast movers (jets).

The first F-105 rolled in on its bomb run and released a CBU (Cluster Bomb Unit) which dispersed hundreds of bomblets about the size of hand grenades right on top of the Hatchet Force. There was dead silence on the radio and then someone said, "Jesus!" After about 30 seconds Don came up on air and reported everyone was ok. The only casualty was a rifle that had been destroyed by a bomblet. The airstrike helped break up an attack by the NVA. More airstrikes broke the NVA's back and they withdrew. LT. Doll estimated that the NVA had more than 100 casualties.

March 1968 was bad for FOB 1. We got a new Commanding Officer, LTC Robert Lopez. He was robust, weighing in at about 200+ pounds, and was missing an index finger. He was enthusiastic and anxious to find ways to get our teams in and out without casualties. He talked to people in camp to get a feel for the operation. We were encouraged by his concern and leadership. His first order of business was to accompany an insertion of a recon team to help him understand some of the problems. Good idea, I thought. He could ride in the chase ship and get a good overview. Right away he nixed that idea, he wanted to be with the team.

I begged him to fly in the chase ship and not in the lift ship. I carefully explained about the density/altitude factor and how critical it was in the mountains in the warm temperatures. His added weight might be enough to bring the helicopter down. He would have none of it. He was going in the lift ship and that was that.

We planned for several days. We would have U.S. Marine CH-46's from HMM-165 for the mission. The pilots wanted to find a box canyon where they could put the nose of the big helicopter down on the trees and hover while the team repelled to the jungle floor.

We found the perfect place and it was well hidden from observation by the ridge lines. Density/altitude was a problem but the pilots thought they could do it. I continued to beg LTC Lopez not to get on the lift ship but he brushed me off like a piece of lint. The pilot, Marine Corps Major William Seward was a really good guy, he looked at me and shrugged his shoulders as if to say, "You tried and I appreciate it." I stepped back and started for the TOC. The choppers lifted off in a cloud of dust.

We were monitoring everything by radio. Things seemed to be going well and the team started to repel to the ground and then Covey relayed that Major Seward reported that he "was losing turns" . . . losing RPM's. Then disaster! The H-46 couldn't hold its hover and it couldn't pull out because our guys were still on the ropes. The big helicopter began settling into the trees. It broke in two and caught fire, coming down on the repelling team members. There was stunned silence in the radio room.

A Jolly Green was over the crash site within the hour and a very brave Para-jumper went down the hoist to rescue the co-pilot and check out the immediate area. He found no additional survivors. LTC. Warren came up from Danang to oversee the situation. I recommended to him that we not put in a "Bright Light (Rescue) Team" until morning. I had been on some "Bright Light" missions where all we accomplished was to get more good men killed or wounded. We thought everyone was accounted for. There were no landing zones nearby and it was going to be dark soon. LTC. Warren concurred. SFC. William McShea did not. Unbeknownst to us, he was on the ground near the crash. He had been on repel and broke his leg when he came down hard during the crash. My decision left him on the ground overnight. I can only imagine what that was like.

I spent longer than usual at the club that evening. The loss was tragic. I went by the TOC on the way to my room. Word was coming in that the co-pilot was out of surgery and telling us there was another survivor. At first light, Covey was over the crash site and had established contact with McShea via mirror flashes. McShea was brought out ASAP. I ran into him at Ft. Bragg sometime later and he assured me that I was not on his Christmas card list. I regret that I put him through that, but I stand by my decision.

Several weeks later another team was on the run. I was the Covey rider. I could see the team coming down the side of a mountain with the NVA in hot pursuit. We had some Huey slicks with McGuire rigs ready to pick them up. McGuire rigs were harnesses on 90 foot ropes dropped from hovering helicopters and used to extract troops from the jungle when there was no place for the helicopters to land.

The team leader, SSG Johnny Calhoun, informed me by radio that he was going to defend in place to slow the NVA down and give his team time to get in the McGuire rigs and get out. He went back up the trail and engaged the on-coming NVA. I was watching from Covey when the NVA reached him and he used his personal grenade to kill himself and several of the NVA. A stunning example of courage and commitment and typical of the kind of men serving at FOB 1.

Another long night at the club. There would be many in the next few months. Casualties mounted. The NVA were everywhere on the Laotian side, helped no doubt by the bombing halt and the war resisters.

At one point the S-3 was tasked to send a man out for a bag of dirt. I wasn't really doing anything at the time so I volunteered. I was briefed that the higher ups wanted a sample of dirt from a particular road junction just inside North Vietnam. I was also given some Psychological-ops material and some Eldest Son ammunition to leave behind. The Psy-Ops material was a pamphlet that NVA Communist Cadre carried that they referred to when lecturing the troops. It had a few notations indicating that some of the things in it weren't true. It was made to look as though a disgruntled Communist Cadre member had made the entries.

Eldest Son was the code name given to a program where we provided booby trapped ammunition to the NVA in various ways. We had evidence that it worked from time to time. Imagine how demoralizing it would be to have no faith in your equipment because you witnessed a mortar round explode in the tube or an AK-47 round blow up in the weapon.

The pilots worked out a route where they would land on a small hill where they would most certainly be seen. Then they would take off and fly down a small valley and drop me off, take off and make another visible landing. Hopefully by making several landings in the area they would confuse or delay the enemy from finding me.

Things were going according to plan and when my stop came they slowed down and I jumped off with my rifle, entrenching tool, a sandbag, a magazine and several loose rounds of Eldest Son AK-47 ammo, and the pamphlet. There was a low ridge between me and the road junction in question. I listened a few minutes before moving over the ridge. I stopped under a bush on the junction side of the ridge and took a long listen. All seemed quiet. I broke off a small tree branch and moved to the edge of the road.

I dropped the magazine under a bush and tossed the loose rounds down the road. I crossed the road and dropped the pamphlet into a bush so it wasn't too obvious. I shoveled about five spades full of dirt into the sand bag and retreated back across the road while wiping out my footsteps with the branch. I made it back to the bush on the side of the ridge and I could hear a helicopter in the distance. I dropped the branch and started over the ridge to rendezvous with my ride home. Perfect! In and out in less than thirty minutes and I didn't get rained on and I made it back to Phu Bai in time for lunch.

Everyone was working their tail off but we didn't catch many breaks. Sometime in May, Major Ratliff, the new FOB 1 Commander, and Captain Walters, the Operations Officer, called me in and explained that Bill Vowel was coming off his Cambodian Battalion job and would be the new Assistant S-3. I could either replace him at the Cambodian Battalion job or become the new S-1 (Administration) Officer. I wasn't ready for this, but orders were orders and two of the most important people in my life would make my decision easy for me.

Bill Vowell, my friend and mentor, was within a few months of completing his tour and I would do everything in my power to keep him safe and see him return to the "Land of the big PX" (home). He more than deserved to come in from the field and if I had to give up a job I liked to make way for him I would do it.

The little blind date girl was my new goal in life. I was almost certain that we would get married. I had even had my Dad purchase an engagement ring for me so that I could propose when I got home. Every night I dreamt of a life of happiness with her and I wanted a chance to make my dreams come true.

I wasn't afraid of combat and actually derived a great deal of satisfaction from some aspects of it. Being an officer and having responsibilities beyond my self-preservation was really rewarding. Coming back from dangerous missions with my unit intact was a point of pride and joy for me. Overcoming mind-numbing fear and moving forward produced a feeling of euphoria that probably exceeded that felt by drug users. My drug was adrenaline and I was addicted. This was my great adventure. However, the little blind date girl occupied my mind at the moment. I wanted her to be my new great adventure.

Even though I knew I wouldn't like it, I chose the S-1 job because I only had a few months left in my tour and the chances of getting home and seeing the little blind date girl were much better if I took the staff job. Major Ratliff and Captain Walters expressed surprise. Apparently I had a decent reputation as a combat commander. They thought I would return to the Cambodian Battalion, but they had never met the little blind date girl. As much as I embraced the thrill and challenge of combat, embracing her was a whole lot better.

XX

I started my time as the Administrative Officer with hope and determination. I wanted to do a good job. The S-1 had lots of responsibilities: personnel actions, awards and decorations, mail, casualty reports, the morning report which accounted for everyone assigned every day, morale, the dispensary, the mess hall, and the indigenous payroll. I was buoyed by the fact that the S-1 shop, under the guidance of SFC Claude Greeney had an excellent staff, and ran day to day on auto-pilot. The Mess Sergeant wasn't in need of my supervision and neither were the medics. If they had a problem, I would help, but they functioned well without my interference. My first morning went well but by lunch I was bored.

Fortunately, I departed for Australia the next week for R&R. I really wanted to go to Australia and had waited 10 months for my turn. Australia was worth the wait. I suffered from a form of reverse culture shock. It was wonderful. The climate was good. It was fall there. It didn't smell like burning shit, there was no danger of being shot at . . . and . . . during my absence from the civilized world, the mini skirt replaced the maxi skirt in women's fashion. I have no words to describe it but I've been a "leg" man ever since.

Someone had advised me not to stay at the beach in July because the temperatures were cool and not many people would be there, so I took a hotel in the banking district of downtown Sidney. Lots of activity during the day but it was not of much interest to me.

The first day I bought a sports coat and a sweater because Australia was famous for their high quality wool and I didn't have any warm clothes.

I went to the movies by myself and watched "The Graduate". It was good but it was about a world I didn't belong to. I began to sense how isolated I was becoming and I was glad I would be heading to the land of the big PX soon (Home).

Most evenings I went to the R&R hotel in the Kings Cross area of Sydney. There was a good bar and guys and girls in micro mini-skirts with whom to talk and dance. I went to a party one night quite by accident. When I was approaching the R&R hotel, I had to step off the sidewalk to make room for a large group of revelers leaving the hotel. A girl reached out and grabbed my arm and said, "Come on. We're going to a party." I lost track of her almost immediately but I had a good time at the party.

Some people started smoking dope and I figured it was time to leave. I was very straight laced. I would drink a little, but rarely to excess. Dope was out of the question. I never wanted to be in a spot where I was not situationally aware and in control of myself. I never wanted to embarrass myself or my family and I was committed to the little blind date girl and would never get into a situation that would incur her disapproval or cause her sadness.

I took a bus tour one day to the forest. It was very different from forests in the U.S. The trees were Eucalyptus Trees. Instead of smelling like pine, the Australian forest smelled like menthol. It was beautiful, not at all like the deserts of Arizona or the jungles of Vietnam.

My last night in Sidney was July 4th and the R&R Center was having a party to celebrate American Independence. I hooked up with a Marine Amtrak Platoon Leader who had put the moves on a cute little gal but was getting hung up because she had come with two girlfriends and he needed a couple of wingmen. We were joined by a Navy guy. We partied until late and the girls split up to take their respective guys home with them. I had to be at the airport in less than three hours to go back to Phu Bai and I hadn't packed yet. And of course there was my absolute devotion to the little blind date girl. Not even a hot blonde Australian girl who was more than a little willing could change my mind. I explained it in the cab. She cried and did the "why can't I find a guy like you?" thing. In the end it was very complementary and I got a peck on the cheek. Was I an idiot? Absolutely. Did I regret it? Maybe just a little bit. I was really glad my first tour in Vietnam was almost over. I had business at home.

About a week after I got back from Australia, I went to Nha Trang to pick up the indigenous pay roll, which was a real pain in the neck. We paid our mercenary troops once a month with local money, piasters and dong. The money was kept in Nha Trang and every month an officer was required to go to Nha Trang by way of Danang and Cam Ranh Bay to pick up and sign for the payroll and return to Phu Bai. It was a week-long detail.

The Air Force had scheduled flights just like an airline. They were called "ass and trash" flights and they were really helpful for moving around the country. I had to chopper down to Danang late in the day and spend the night. The next morning I caught a ride to the big airfield and got on a C-130 to Cam Ranh Bay. I got on another C-130 to Nha Trang. Spent another night there to account for the money the next day and fly back, spending the night in Danang. Upon arrival in Phu Bai the next morning, we paid all the indigenous troops and workers which took all day. We paid them in groups and had Americans in attendance to vouch for them. I knew the Cambodians, but had to have someone who knew the Nungs, the day-laborers, the maids, and the office workers to help verify their legitimacy. In addition we injected a miniscule amount of India ink under their cuticles so they couldn't come back through in a different group.

For the next two days I took the money and paperwork back to Danang and spent most of the day doing the accounting. It is a skill they don't teach in infantry training and I was thankful for the Finance Officer assigned to assist me. He looked the part; wire-rimmed glasses, little moustache, and the hands and fingers of a pianist, (probably so he could count money faster), all that was missing was an eye shade and sleeve garters. He was a good guy and when we got done we had dinner and a couple of drinks at the Club. He went to the movie and I went to find my room.

Turned out I had to share the room with a Major who shall remain nameless. His tour was over and he was heading home. His Army Dress Green uniform was hanging on the front of a wall locker resplendent with the ribbons and badges denoting a hardened combat veteran who had seen more action than most. It was damned impressive!

Said Major came into the room a few minutes later and we greeted each other. I knew him slightly because he was assigned to FOB 1 and had been there for my entire tour. He was in good spirits because he had been into the good spirits most of the afternoon. Even though we had shared ten months in the same camp I hardly knew him. I knew he was a body builder and lifted weights almost every day but to me he was a ghost. On paper he was assigned as the Commanding Officer of FOB 1 but he shared that with Maj Ira Snell. Snell took command and the unnamed Major sort of disappeared, only to re-emerge when it was time for him to go home. He was a happy drunk and decided to mentor me on how to become a successful Army Officer. Obviously he didn't know me from Adam.

We started with his uniform and he showed me the patches and badges representing some of the training he had been through. I had already been through most of what he talked about and I was proud of my training too, but I couldn't get a word in edgewise so I nodded a lot.

Then we moved to the awards and decorations displayed on his "going home" uniform. He emphasized how important it was for Officer's to get the "right" medals and he pointed to his Silver Star, the third highest valor award that the nation could confer on a combat soldier. He also said it was important to have complimentary medals like the Purple Heart which he also had along with a Bronze Star for Combat Service. He told me the story about how he rescued the pilot of an Air Force rescue helicopter and how the pilot received the Medal of Honor. I had my suspicions.

Thankfully he was getting tired and fell asleep after our stroll through his glory. I, on the other hand, was awake most of the night because I was mad as hell. I had never seen the man leave camp the whole time I was there. As far as I know, he did not see a day of combat. I had spent the last nine months in combat and flying Covey and had no medals at all other than an Army Commendation Medal which was the lowest level award that was given. We called it the "Green Weeny" because it was one step above nothing. Frankly, I was embarrassed that I had no medals of consequence to pin on my "going home" uniform.

A few weeks later I checked the records on Major Ghost and was no longer mad . . . I was furious! As I suspected, he had claimed his Silver Star and Purple Heart for the mission I led to find Jolly Green 26 and rescue any and all survivors. I overlooked the Purple Heart because he may have gotten a paper cut or dropped a weight on his toe during that period but the Silver Star was an insult to all of us who served with honor and integrity. Years later, he stopped claiming to have earned a Silver Star. I guess somebody called him on it.

Back at Phu Bai, I slipped into the daily administrative routines. Nothing too taxing and Bill Vowell would sometimes offer me an opportunity to get out and pretend I was still a war fighter. One day we were flying over Ashau Valley in a Vietnamese Air Force Cessna 182, watching the ground looking for targets and serving as a radio relay for a recon team that needed us while their Covey was off station (not in the area). Bill lit up C-ration Pall-Mall and when he was done, he dropped it into the hole where an ashtray had once been.

A minute or two later we smelled smoke and it was getting hazy in the cabin. Then we saw fire. We gave each other a wide-eyed look and I know Bill was thinking the same thing I was. We were about to become a fireball and plunge into the middle of Ashau Valley in a last glorious effort to bring the opportunity for democracy to the peoples of South Vietnam. The pilots were also giving each other wide-eyed looks until the co-pilot calmly reached back with a small fire extinguisher and put out the fire. We returned to Phu Bai post haste.

I spent the last weeks of my first tour in Vietnam filing forms and writing awards. Sometimes writing the awards was a real pleasure and I put some real work into trying to capture the undeniable courage and professionalism of the men I knew as brothers. Other awards were for the ghost Majors and senior Captains who needed help with their careers. Those efforts depressed me, but at the end of the day I would get to sit down and write the little blind date girl and that always lifted my spirits.

Eventually Bill went home, Chips extended and went to Khe Sanh, "Top" Fisher and Team A-323 returned to Okinawa and I was alone in a camp of strangers filling up with new age soldiers that had no use for me. I was the S-1, a background player.

Eventually it was September and time to go home, but I hadn't received any orders transferring me home. As the S-1, I was able to straighten the problem out quickly. I talked to someone at Infantry Branch back in the States and he initially told me I wasn't in the Army and he had no record of me. I told him to keep looking. Eventually my jacket (file) turned up. It had been filed as missing in action.

He apologized and said he was tele-typing orders ASAP but that I was unassigned so after I'd had thirty days leave I could call him and he would assign me wherever I wanted to go. Sweet! The orders came the next morning and I started packing!

My "Freedom Bird" was a contract DC-8 Seaboard World airliner configured in the cattle car seating arrangement. It was packed with guys who looked more hopeful than happy. I left with mixed feelings. I no longer had any illusions about the war and was excited to be heading home to my family and the little blind date girl, but my brothers were here and they were still fighting. I didn't want to leave them and I was already suffering from survivor's remorse.

We taxied to the end of the runway and the big jet turned to align itself with the center line, the engines powered up and in moments we were flying. I expected to hear cheers and celebration but it wasn't like that at all. Dead silence. As we left the ground I sensed a release of held breaths. I sat there dumbfounded. I was going home to my family and the little blind date girl. The mixed feeling of joy and sorrow was inexplicable. We all strained for our last look at the "Nam".

We faced eighteen hours of travel in cramped quarters. I'm sure everyone's thoughts turned to home but it didn't take me long to go back. So much had happened in the last year. For me personally even the bad was good, it taught me things I could not have learned anywhere or anyway else. What an incredible, death defying, culturally enlightening experience I had been given.

When the United States entered World War II, FDR delivered the famous "Day that shall live in infamy" speech to Congress in which he said, "We have nothing to fear but fear itself!" I think he was right. I had seen fear send men running, or worse frozen them in place. Fear is a reaction; courage is a choice. I had faced fear that felt like a cold icicle stabbing me in the heart and prevailed. Although the fear could be paralyzing in many people, I always reacted the same way. I was responsible for the people around me and I acted accordingly. What wonderful people they were. Mostly I thought about the people; the Cambodians and the Nungs so loyal and brave and the Vietnamese people who really just wanted to be left in peace and would have been if it weren't for politicians and governments.

And the Americans, my God what great men some of them were. Far too many men in SOG died trying to bring back important real-time intelligence which, more than likely, was disregarded. The whole experience was a gift and I had survived it. I thought about the things that had changed, there weren't many, and I realized that the politicians were neutralized by their ambition and fear of offending the anti-war movement and losing votes. And I realized that the generals were neutralized by their sense of duty and fear of the politicians. Nothing was changing. We were fighting to maintain the status quo and our leaders had no exit plan. I knew I would go back to Vietnam because of my sense of duty and my love for my brothers who were still fighting there.

We flew for hours and flew into the night. My thoughts bounced back and forth from what I had left behind to what lay ahead. I remembered back to the first memorial service I attended at FOB 1. We had a circuit riding Chaplin whose principal job seemed to be traveling among the Forward Operating Bases saying good-bye to our dead. I was very moved by his first sermon where he talked about our men drinking from the challis of courage too many times. I thought it really described our situation, but then I heard the same thing ten days later and two weeks after that and by the fourth or fifth time my senses were dulled and I didn't want to hear it anymore, but the Chaplin kept coming and I kept attending out of respect for the men who had given their lives.

Then I thought of home and my future. There was so much to look forward to.

Our first refueling stop on the way home was Yokota Air Base in Japan. As we reduced speed and started our let down, the pilot came on the intercom and advised us that there was a problem with one of the landing gears. He thought everything would be ok but as a precaution he was declaring an emergency. Great! I just survived a year in a combat zone and now I would die in a plane crash on the way home.

As we landed, several fire trucks raced along-side the plane but we had landed safely and taxied to the terminal. We were delayed several hours while a new part was flown in. Most of the businesses in the terminal were closed and it was boring. I tried to get some sleep but I was way too keyed up. Finally we re-boarded and departed for Anchorage, Alaska. After a quick refueling we were off to Seattle. Even though we were "home" we had to fly all the way to Ft. Dix, New Jersey to clear Customs and out process.

It was early morning when we arrived at Ft. Dix. We carried our belongings into a long shed while a scratchy recording of Marshall Music played over the intercom. We were met by a bunch of bored MP's who searched our stuff. We repacked our belongings and were free to go on leave. No one welcomed us home or helped us find transportation to an airport or train station. It was not a homecoming. It was the first of many insults that I would endure as a returning soldier from Vietnam. I was baffled by my country's attitude toward its military members.

I took a Shuttle Bus to the Philadelphia Airport and bought a ticket on American Airlines to Tucson by way of Dallas and Phoenix. In Dallas I got a shave at the terminal barber shop and was immediately taken back to Phu Bai. An old Vietnamese barber would come into the camp once a week to cut our hair. He had no electric shavers so he used scissors and hand clippers which pulled out as much hair as they cut. I never got comfortable with the old gentleman holding a straight razor to my neck, but at the end of the haircut he would massage my neck. Sitting in the warm sun getting a neck massage was really relaxing and I always looked forward to it.

Finally I changed planes in Phoenix for the last leg of my journey. Flying into Tucson, I was looking down at the desert and thinking it looked like the surface of Mars after spending a year flying over lush jungles and beautiful emerald green rice paddies. But I loved my desert and could hardly wait to get home to it.

We landed and I made my way to the terminal and there was Dad, Mom and my brothers. What a sight for sore eyes and I realized how hard the year must have been for my parents. I quickly looked around and there she was, the little blind date girl, the woman I would love for the rest of my life, all ninety-eight pounds, five-foot-two-inches of her. It was the most perfect moment of my life.

Linda Matkins and I were married on November 17, 1968. I returned to Vietnam on November 14, 1969. I was the Company Commander of Charlie Company, 2/18th, 1st Infantry Division. My personal mission was to see all my soldiers got home in one piece.

I accomplished my mission.

Made in the USA
Middletown, DE
10 September 2024

60725687R00142